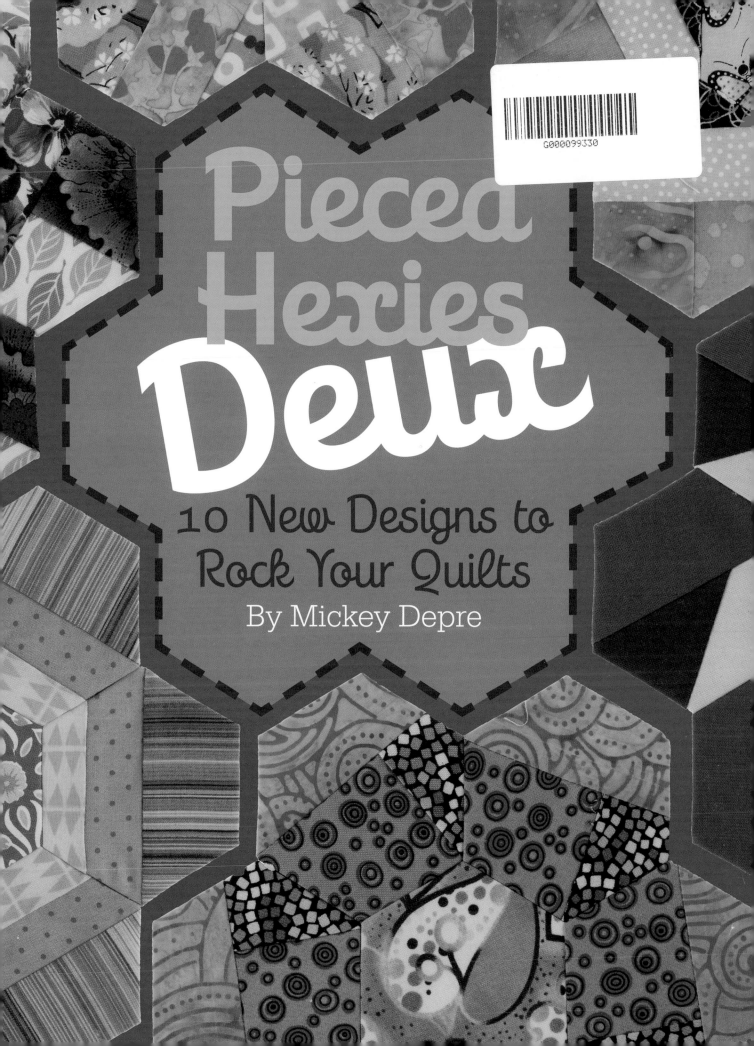

Pieced Hexies Deux

10 New Designs to Rock Your Quilts

By Mickey Depre

Pieced Hexies Deux

10 New Designs to Rock Your Quilts

By Mickey Depre

Editor: Deb Rowden
Designer: Kelly Ludwig
Photography: Aaron T. Leimkuehler
Illustration: Eric Sears
Technical Editor: Christina DeArmond
Photo Editor: Jo Ann Groves

Published by:
Kansas City Star Books
1729 Grand Blvd.
Kansas City, Missouri, USA 64108

First edition, first printing
ISBN: 978-0-9604884-1-4

Library of Congress Control Number: 2013956000

Printed in the United States of America by Walsworth Publishing Co., Marceline, MO

To order copies, call StarInfo at (816) 234-4473.

Contents

Dedication / Acknowledgement

Graduation - Hendrix College, Conway, Arkansas, 2013

It **only seems appropriate that** this second book of Pieced Hexies designs is dedicated to the other set of "twos" in my life: my children—Paul Jr., and Emily—by far, my greatest creations.

The year 2013 included college graduation, a major stepping stone for all four of us, as Paul Sr. and I are now true empty nesters. Working on this book during the summer provided this mother with the void-filler that allowed her now adult children the ability to do things their way without my well-intended, but probably not needed, input.

With that, I would like to give special thanks to Doug Weaver for his unknown foresight to schedule such timely publication.

And to Deb Rowden, my editor, who dealt with my crazy hours and sometimes rambling, panicked phone calls as she pulled it all together yet again for me. She worked her magic and jammed more material into this book then I believed possible. You are truly the best, Deb!

To my team at Kansas City Star Quilts who always make my work and books look fantastic: Kelly Ludwig, Aaron Leimkuehler, Eric Sears, Christina DeArmond, and Jo Ann Groves—thank you.

About the Author

Mickey Depre was introduced to the world of fiber arts by her own personal "grandmasters" at the age of four. Grandmothers, great aunts, aunts and her mother filled her days with cloth, needles, yarn, and such.

Textiles, from vintage to current, have always fascinated her and her taste has always been for ALL! Sewing in general—mending to garment-making—is never a chore.

In 1997, Mickey found quilting on her own. She is the first quiltmaker in her family, but vows not to be the only one.

Chicago has been her lifelong home. Married to her high school sweetheart, Paul, they are the proud parents of a set of grown twins, Paul Jr. and Emily. Molly, their miniature dachshund, now fills their "nest" with joy.

Mickey has quietly instilled her love of sewing into all their lives: husband, son, and daughter can all sew (it's a bit rough for Molly to reach the pedal so she is working on ironing skills). She is now waiting for one of them to want to share her stash.

Mickey enjoys sharing her love of fiber through lectures and workshops. Her workshops mix technique instruction with individual creativity (and always a giggle or two). You can find more information at www.mdquilts.com.

Pieced Hexies Deux is Mickey's third publication with Kansas City Star Quilts. You can find more Pieced Hexie designs in *Pieced Hexies: A New Tradition in English Paper Piecing* and *Ring Around the Hexies*.

Introduction

*A*blank page.

That's what I see as I sit in my hometown library, staring at my laptop screen. It is a rare Saturday at home and I have only two pages to tell you all about *Pieced Hexies Deux*. Where to start? Oh my, there is so much to tell.

This year has been another whirlwind for me. As I sit staring at this blank page with a moment to gather all my thoughts, I keep coming back to the over-used but absolutely fitting quote by Sally Field at the 1984 Oscars (slightly revised to fit this scenario):

"You like them (Pieced Hexies), you really like them!"

These simple designs are like potato chips—you start with one, and you just can't stop. You may even find yourself spinning them around in your head as you close your eyes to fall asleep. (I have gotten the emails, the Facebook messages, I hear you, I am sorry about the lack of sleep.)

We present **ten new designs** to play with. Eleven, if you count the 50/50 design used in some of the *Pieced Hexies Deux* Stars.

Take a look at the very first design in the book—Lanes. Lanes is first because I chose to do things a bit different this time around. A first book is much like the first year of a new car model: it is a learning experience. I learned a lot, such as:

⊗ To make room for more illustrations and designs, I decided to include **recoloring variations** with only one design (see Lanes, page 15). I hope by seeing this method that you, my very savvy quilter, will let your imagination apply this idea to the other designs in the book. Take a moment and explore how recoloring works, then apply this concept to all the other designs (and the hundreds, if not thousands of variations still to be created using Pieced Hexies).

⊗ I added **letter labels in the corners** of each Hexie (A-F) for added clarity when marking the alignment guidelines on your papers. And yes, there is a template set available for Deux (see Resources, page 96). Note that the templates are not necessary to make any of my designs—I will always provide pencil and ruler instructions. Templates are tools to make the process easier and faster if you choose to use them.

My students asked for the **Fabric Orientation Guides** to show where the fabrics in the 3 ½" blocks are placed when transferred to the Hexie shape.

Take special note for these designs: Boxed, Buzzsaw, Chop, Kilter, Layer and Scissors. These are non-symmetrical quilt blocks, so you mark your alignment guides in reverse. See page 42 for a complete explanation. If there is one slight stumbling block in the technique of Pieced Hexies, this is it—nonsymmetrical designs. Once you understand the concept, you will be fine.

As before, I have included **Combo Designs**. Eighteen! Again, this is just a drop in the bucket of the variations possible when you use two different Pieced Hexies to make a traditional rosette.

I hope you use my Pieced Hexies books as **reference tools** much like the classic block books of years past – a resource for creating a very original Hexie project. I chose not to include specific quilt patterns as these Pieced Hexies can be applied to any and every English Paper Piecing pattern that is already in print. As you can imagine, the variations are truly in the millions when an individual chooses the design they like best and begins to twirl those Pieced Hexies around.

After the publication of my first book, the idea of **Pieced Hexies Stars** was born. I created six for my website (mdquilts.com) as free PDFs using designs from the first book. The Stars are named after women in my life or in a few cases, with names I have always loved. These stars can be incorporated into a full Hexie quilt, or used as applique motifs, either on a whole cloth background or a pieced background. Again, the choice is yours.

Six Stars are included in this book: Diane, Bonnie, Elaine, Cathy, Linda, and Maggie.

We've included a black/white line drawing of each star for you to photocopy and color based on your fabric choices. You'd better make multiple copies if you are like me. I find myself coloring and recoloring these pages.

Be sure to watch my website for future Pieced Hexies Star patterns that use designs from both books.

So! Now my page is not blank anymore. My wheels are spinning in so many creative directions as I look over the designs. I hope yours are too.

Hex On!

Mickey

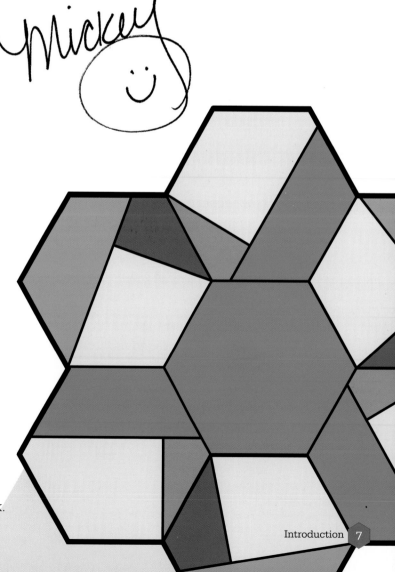

Look for combos like these scattered throughout the book.

General Supplies

First and foremost … from here on, a paper Hexagon will be referred to as a Hexie.

Just the FAQs ma'am.

What exactly is a Hexie?

Hexie is my nickname for a English Paper Piecing Hexagon shape (any size). You can buy these papers in die cut packs at your local quilt shop or you can print them out using your computer and heavyweight paper at home. If you cut them out yourself, take your time and be precise so your Hexies finish at the proper size. There are several websites that have Hexie pdfs/jpegs that you can download for printing (see Resources, page 96).

What size Hexie do I need to make the patterns in this book?

All the patterns in this book are made using an 1 ½" Hexie. Hexies are referred to by the length of one edge of the shape. Thus, every edge is 1 ½" on a 1 ½" Hexie. The center measurement or width of any Hexie is twice the edge length. So a 1 ½" Hexie is 3" wide. But note: a Hexie is **not** as tall as it is wide. Due to the nature of the shape, they are a bit on the short side. A 1 ½" Hexie is only 2 ⅝" tall.

What size piece of fabric do I need to cover my Hexie?

All the patterns in this book are made using a 3 ½" pieced fabric square and basted to a Hexie. There is a little bit of waste but it is easier to piece a 3 ½" square than a 3 ½" x 3 ⅛" rectangle. Sometimes a little waste is ok. Based on this, I also cut 3 ½" squares for the centers of my Pieced Hexie Rosettes.

Do I need a special needle?

Actually I recommend two.

I like John James self-threading needle for basting. This needle has a little lever on the top so all you have to do is hold your basting thread over it, tug down, and voila! Your needle and thread are ready to go.

To sew Hexies together, I like a fine milliner's needle. A pack of Richard Hemming and Son Milliners size 11 can always be found in my sewing box. The size is up to you. Try starting off with a larger needle for ease if you are new to handwork. Once you feel comfortable, scale down to a finer needle for more delicate stitches.

What happens if I have difficulty threading my hand needle?

I highly recommend the purchase of a needle threader. I would be lost without my Clover table top threader in my arsenal of tools.

And thread - what about thread?

This is a sticky wicket. Experiment! My current favorites are listed below, but I am always trying new threads and have found that sometimes certain threads work better with certain types of cotton. And of course you need different threads - just like needles - for different jobs.

For basting, I use leftover thread. See, you have now found a use for that half spool of blaring orange leftover from your pumpkin costume. Remember, basting thread is just temporary so any color goes.

To sew Hexies together, I go back and forth between a fine silk thread (YLI brand) doubled for strength, and a 60 weight cotton thread (Presencia). I find that both give me the ability to hide stitches as they sink nicely into the fabrics. I use silk thread when working with batiks and hand-dyed fabrics. They usually have a tight weave due to being prewashed. So now you have figured out I don't prewash my cottons ... that is a whole other obsession, and I don't care to go there.

How about some protection for my fingertip?

I use a thimble, a leather coin thimble to be exact. Experiment here too and find what feels most comfortable for you. Remember that some thimbles (i.e. leather ones) take a bit of time and use to break in and fit properly so don't make a thimble choice too hastily.

Pins? Can one ever have enough pins?

I use a fine long shafted pin for my Hexies. 'Nuff said.

Can I run with my scissors?

No, I never condone running with scissors. Miss Schrage, my kindergarten teacher, drilled that into my head. But I do love a good pair of scissors. For this project, you might want to have two different blades close by. A pair of fabric cutting scissors for trimming your 3 ½" square when you are basting and a pair of small embroidery scissors that can easily tuck into your on-the-go-box/bag for use. Hexies are wonderful on-the-go projects and great conversation starters at ball games, doctor offices, school functions (oh how I wish I was making Hexies when I attended years of band performances ... the projects I could have had completed ...).

Why piece a rosette?

My Hexie journey started with the traditional rosette because that was what I saw in patterns everywhere. Most of the samples in the book are done in the rosette style. But that is just the tip of the design iceberg for Pieced Hexies. I see chevron quilts, border treatments, and a multitude of other applications ... let your imagination run wild.

English Paper Piecing Instructions

What's an On-the-Go box/bag?

Simple. A collection of all the items necessary to baste or sew together a few Hexies in those snippets of time we all have in our daily lives. Besides the examples stated above: on the train, lunch break, coffee break, and especially at night when you are watching TV or listening to some music. Hexies are great friends too as your hands are busy with them instead of reaching for the chip bowl. Just sayin'.

Do you ever have to "unsew"?

Yes it happens all the time. Unsewing is basically what you will do when you are removing the basting from your Hexie after all six sides have been stabilized or connected to another hexagon. To do this, you need a good sharp seam ripper. Check my resource guide (page 96) for information regarding beautiful hand-turned handle seam rippers. It is nice to have at least one of these to call your own.

Basic Basting

1. Place your selected fabric on the table in front of you with the wrong side facing up.

2. Pin your paper to the fabric allowing at least ¼" around all edges.

3. Trim the fabric, leaving a ¼" seam. Use your paper for guidance regarding the shape.

4. Fold the excess fabric over the paper piece and baste using a large running stitch around all the edges. Fold the corner inward like a mitered binding and make sure your basting stitches run over each corner to hold the folded fabric flat and stable.

The Sewing Together

1. Hold 2 Hexies together, right sides touching, and edges lined up.

2. Knot the end of your sewing thread.

3. Run your needle about ½" from the corner of your edge. This will place your knot away from the corner and will reduce bulk.

4. Take 2 stitches in the corner to secure it. You want your small whip stitches to just catch the edges of the fabric. Try not to sew through the paper. You may nick it a few times when you first start out. Don't worry, it's ok.

5. This is when I do things a little bit differently. After the initial first couple of whip stitches, I open up the Hexies so that they lay flat in my hand and continue to sew. I gently run the needle through the fabric and across the paper. Think buttonhole stitch without the carrying of the thread across. No stitches show on the front of the Hexies for a crisp, clean appearance.

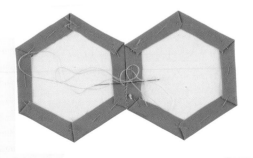

6. When I reach the opposite corner, I add another Hexie. Make sure to really secure those corners by double stitching at the end of one side and at the beginning of another or later you may find small openings or holes where your Hexies meet.

7. When you either run out of thread or Hexies, it's time to knot off. Run your needle back towards the center of an edge length again (as you did to start) and then knot off. Again keep your corners as bulk free as possible.

8. When all sides of a Hexie have been stabilized/sewn to another, remove the basting threads and the paper Hexie from the back. The paper piece can be used again.

Pieced Hexie Basting Instructions

Now that you've learned about English Paper Piecing, let's tailor that style to Pieced Hexie paper piecing.

It is my preference to use needle and thread to baste Hexies. It keeps the seams from shifting out of alignment. When stitching over the folded corners, keep them as flat as possible. You can use a gluestick for basting if you prefer. The choice is yours but give the following method a try, at least once. Sometimes "old school" is best.

An Echo block (page 22) is shown in these pictures. Remember, these instructions can be applied to any of the designs in the book.

It is important to trim your seam allowances to a scant ⅛" immediately after sewing every seam. With this is mind, I suggest you change your stitch number to slightly smaller than your default for a tighter stitch. If you forget to trim as you sew, don't worry. Just trim before basting.

⊗ Pieced Hexie designs are based on each paper hexagon being covered with a simple pieced 3 ½" square.

⊗ Turn the pieced block so the wrong side is facing you.

⊗ You must use a 1 ½" size hexagon for this method. This measurement is the length of each side. The center width measurement of this hexagon is 3". The height measurement is 2 ⅝".

⊗ Following the individual instructions given in each pattern section, draw alignment guidelines on your hexagon.

⊗ Place the paper hexagon with drawn guidelines on top of the pieced 3 ½" square. Line up the drawn guidelines with the **seam** lines.

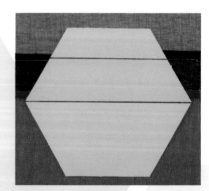

⊛ Pin the paper hexagon in place. Use a pin with a longer shaft and put at least ¾" to 1" of space between pin holes to keep the hexagon as flat as possible.

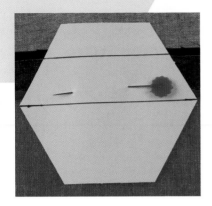

⊛ Trim excess fabric away, leaving a generous ¼" around the hexagon. Note that at the center points, the seam allowance might be slightly smaller.

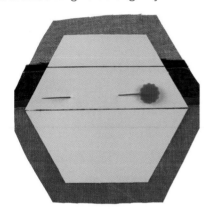

⊛ Begin your running basting stitch on an edge that contains a seam so you can secure it immediately. Tuck in excess material on the corners like you would to miter bind on a quilt or make a bed. Be sure to make a stitch over the fold created as you move from one side of the hexagon to the next.

⊛ This hexagon lays flat with all the corner folds held down with a running stitch over them. On the final fold, make 2 running stitches over the fold in the shape of a plus sign. Draw the thread one last half stitch to the back and clip. No need to knot at the end - the double stitching will hold the basting stitch in place.

⊛ This is your basted Pieced Hexie from the front. Only five more to go to make a Hexie rosette!

Symmetrical
Designs

Lanes

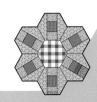

Be sure to read General Supplies, English Paper Piecing Instructions, and Pieced Hexie Basting Instructions before you start.

These instructions are for piecing 6 – 3 ½" squares for each rosette. The center hexagon is a solid fabric. No piecing instructions are needed: just use a 3 ½" square.

Fabric Orientation Guide

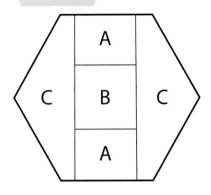
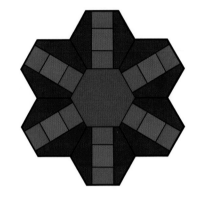
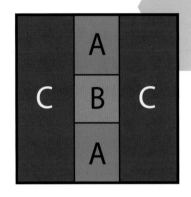

Material Needed for 1 Square

- ✪ Fabric A: (2) 1 ½" x 1 ½"
- ✪ Fabric B: 1 ½" x 1 ½"
- ✪ Fabric C: (2) 1 ½" x 3 ½"

Fabric Preparation

- ✪ Sew A to the lengthwise edge of B.
- ✪ Sew an A/B unit lengthwise with the edge of B to a second A.

OR

Material Needed for 6 Squares

- ✪ Fabric A: (2) 1 ½" x 10"
- ✪ Fabric B: 1 ½" x 10"
- ✪ Fabric C: (12) 1 ½" x 3 ½"

Fabric Preparation

Important: trim pieced seams to ⅛" after each one is sewn. This will reduce bulk for basting.

- ✪ Sew the strips together lengthwise in an A-B-A pattern.
- ✪ Cut the A-B-A strip into 1 ½" segments.

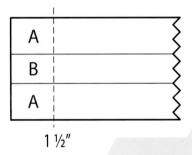

1 ½"

- ✪ Sew C to each lengthwise side of an A-B-A segment.

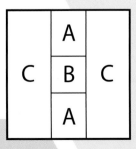

3 ½" Lanes sewn square

Paper Preparation

Baste the sewn square to the paper pattern. Perfect alignment is important; mark your paper hexagon with the alignment guides shown. Use a sharp pointed pencil or fine tip pen to mark lines. To mark accurately, angle your marking instrument tip into the groove of the ruler and paper.

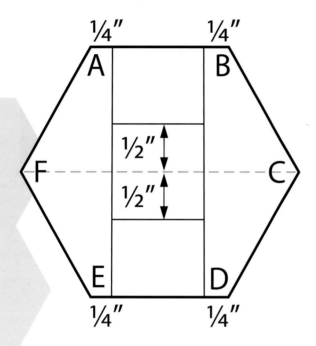

Lanes Alignment Guides

Note: For this symmetrical block, place a paper Hexie in front of you and label the corners (A through F) as shown on the guide.

- ✹ Measure ¼" to the right of points A and E and draw a vertical guideline.

- ✹ Measure ¼" to the left of points B and D and draw a vertical guideline.

- ✹ Measuring from the center point (points F and C across), draw a guideline between the 2 previous drawn lines, ½" above the center, and ½" below the center. This will create a 1" square box floating in the center of your Hexie.

Assembly

- ✹ Place the sewn square with the seam side facing up.

- ✹ Place the marked paper pattern on top of the sewn square with markings facing up.

- ✹ Line up the sewn seams and paper marks. *Note: Push a pin through one or 2 of the corners of the center square to line up with drawn guideline square. Carefully pin once in the center, securing the sewn square to the paper.*

- ✹ Trim away excess fabric, leaving a generous ¼" on each side for basting.

- ✹ Baste the sewn square to the paper hexagon, using a running stitch. *Start your basting on an edge with a seam to secure.*

- ✹ **Do not** remove the pin until at least 3 sides are basted.

Note: In the following pages, we show variations achieved by recoloring a repetitive fabric section in a design. These recolorings have a "B" in their name.

This method of creative play can be applied to other designs in this book (but will not be shown). As you can see, these variations are just a hint of the possibilities! But we have to keep this book at a reasonable size (no one wants to carry around a 300 page quilt book), so just a few are shown.

Let your imagination play—see what you discover when you twist, turn, and recolor!

Lanes Original A

Mic's Musings: *The smallest part of this design—the center block—is the most dynamic part. Make sure the fabric you choose to place there can be seen.*

Mic's Musings: *The Fabric C switch can be either bold or subtle. The trick is finding what works best with your other fabric choices.*

Lanes Original B / Recolored

Lanes Variation 1A

Mic's Musings: *In this design, you can use a larger scale print successfully because fabric A is repeated so much.*

Mic's Musings: *Choose a brand new color for added splash when recoloring!*

Lanes Variation 1B / Recolored

Lanes Variation 2A

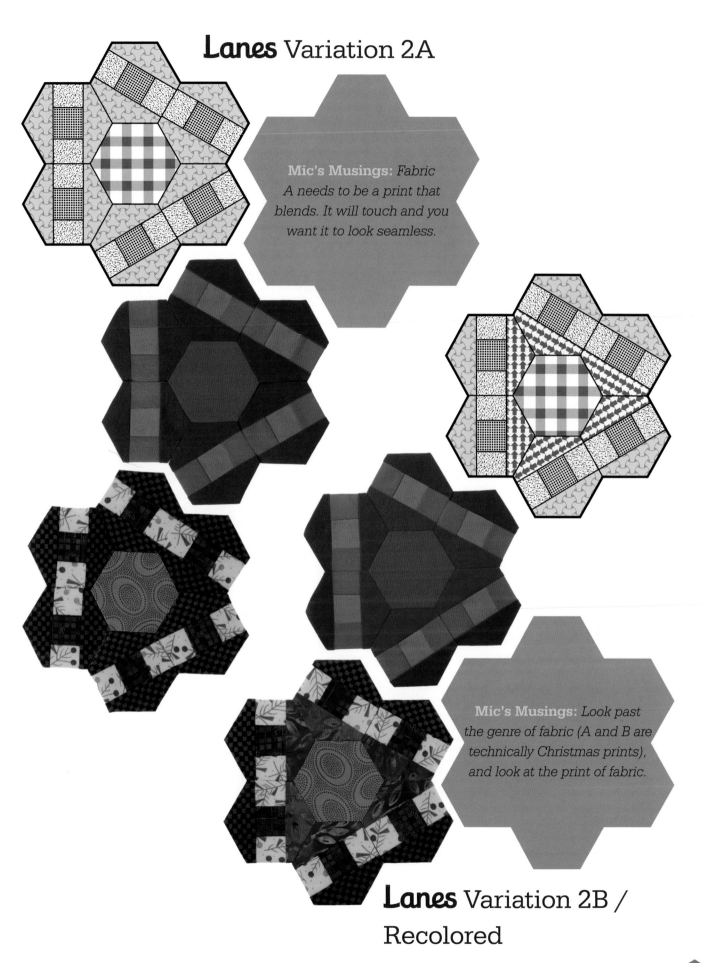

Mic's Musings: *Fabric A needs to be a print that blends. It will touch and you want it to look seamless.*

Mic's Musings: *Look past the genre of fabric (A and B are technically Christmas prints), and look at the print of fabric.*

Lanes Variation 2B / Recolored

Lanes Variation 3A

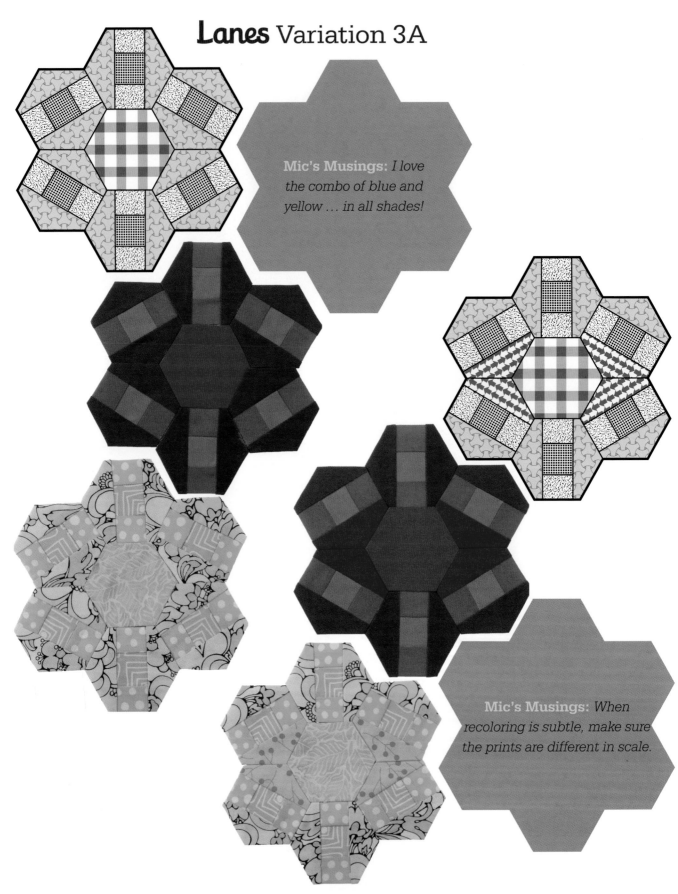

Mic's Musings: *I love the combo of blue and yellow … in all shades!*

Mic's Musings: *When recoloring is subtle, make sure the prints are different in scale.*

Lanes Variation 3B / Recolored

Lanes Variation Bonus

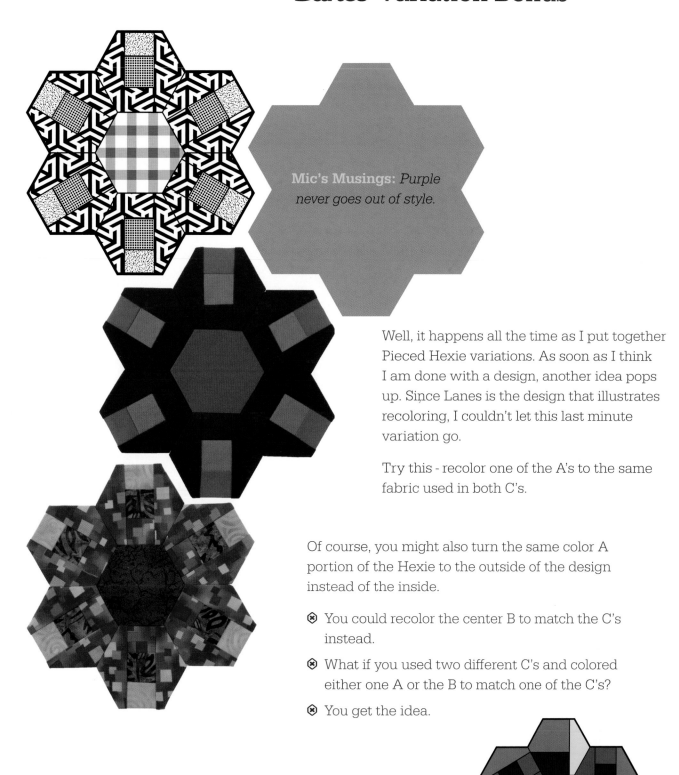

Mic's Musings: *Purple never goes out of style.*

Well, it happens all the time as I put together Pieced Hexie variations. As soon as I think I am done with a design, another idea pops up. Since Lanes is the design that illustrates recoloring, I couldn't let this last minute variation go.

Try this - recolor one of the A's to the same fabric used in both C's.

Of course, you might also turn the same color A portion of the Hexie to the outside of the design instead of the inside.

⊛ You could recolor the center B to match the C's instead.

⊛ What if you used two different C's and colored either one A or the B to match one of the C's?

⊛ You get the idea.

Echo

Be sure to read General Supplies, English Paper Piecing Instructions, and Pieced Hexie Basting Instructions before you start.

These instructions are for piecing 6 – 3 ½" squares for each rosette. The center hexagon is a solid fabric. No piecing instructions are needed: just use a 3 ½" square.

Fabric Orientation Guide

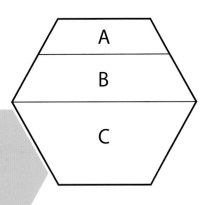

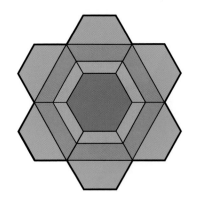

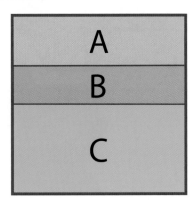

Material Needed for 1 Square

- ✻ Fabric A: 1 ¼" x 3 ½"
- ✻ Fabric B: 1 ¼" x 3 ½"
- ✻ Fabric C: 2" x 3 ½"

Fabric Preparation

- ✻ Sew A to the lengthwise edge of B.
- ✻ Sew A/B unit lengthwise with the edge of B to C.

OR

Material Needed for 6 Squares

- ✻ Fabric A: 1 ¼" x 22"
- ✻ Fabric B: 1 ¼" x 22"
- ✻ Fabric C: 2" x 22"

Fabric Preparation

Important: Trim pieced seams to ⅛" after each one is sewn. This will reduce bulk for basting.

- ✻ Sew the strips together lengthwise in an A-B pattern. Press the seam toward fabric A.

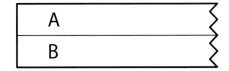

- ✻ Sew an A-B strip lengthwise with the edge of B to C.
- ✻ Cut the A-B-C strip into 3 ½" segments to make finished 3 ½" squares.

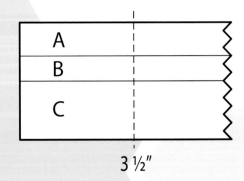

3 ½"

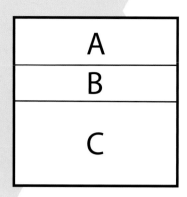

3 ½" Echo sewn square

Paper Preparation

Baste the sewn square to the paper pattern. Perfect alignment is important; mark your paper hexagon with the alignment guides shown. Use a sharp pointed pencil or fine tip pen to mark lines. To mark accurately, angle your marking instrument tip into the groove of the ruler and paper.

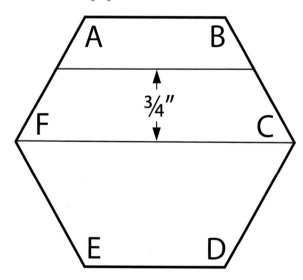

Echo Alignment Guides

Note: For this symmetrical block, place a paper Hexie in front of you and label the corners (A through F) as shown on the guide.

- ✸ Draw a guideline through the center horizontally from corner F to corner C.

- ✸ Draw a second guideline spaced ¾" from the first drawn line from edge to edge.

Assembly

- ✸ Place the sewn square with the seam side facing up.

- ✸ Place the marked paper pattern on top of the sewn square with markings facing up.

- ✸ Line up the sewn seams and paper marks. Carefully pin once in the center, securing the sewn square to the paper.

- ✸ Trim away excess fabric, leaving a generous ¼" on each side for basting.

- ✸ Baste the sewn square to the paper hexagon, using a running stitch. *Start your basting on an edge with a seam to secure.*

- ✸ **Do not** remove the pin until at least 3 sides are basted.

Echo Original

Mic's Musings: *Use fabrics with patterns that radiate outward for impact.*

Mic's Musings: *Make sure your scale of print fits the section where you place it. In this example, the cherry print needed the largest area so the cherries could be seen.*

Echo Variation 1

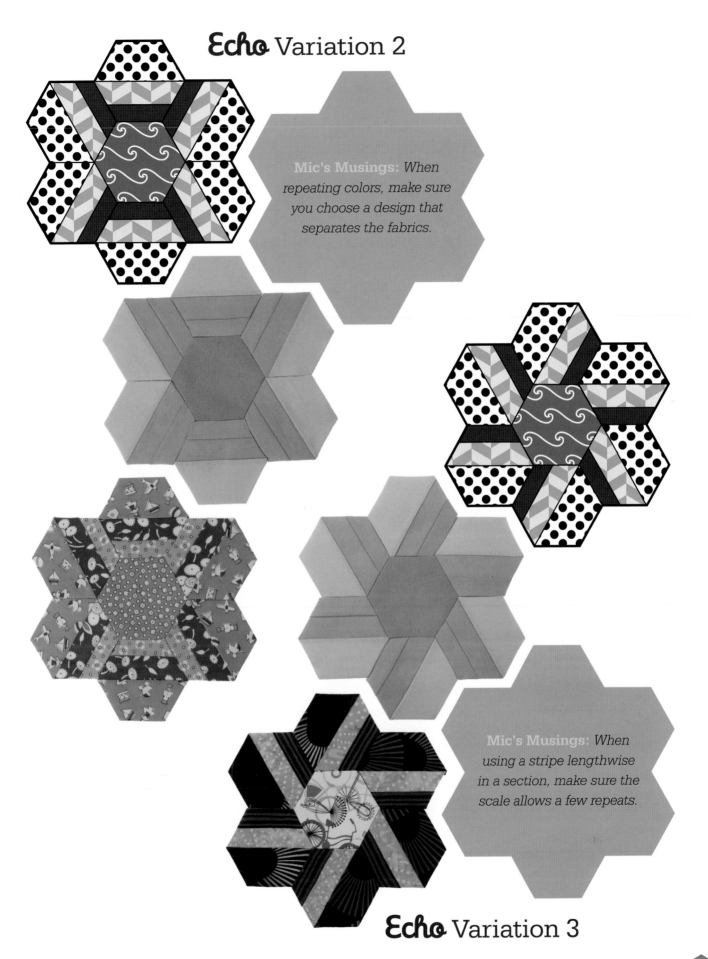

Echo Variation 2

Mic's Musings: *When repeating colors, make sure you choose a design that separates the fabrics.*

Mic's Musings: *When using a stripe lengthwise in a section, make sure the scale allows a few repeats.*

Echo Variation 3

Echo Variation 4

Mic's Musings: *Don't get stuck in the "it-has-to-match" rut ... sometimes, just going with your gut (like this center) can be exciting.*

Mic's Musings: *In this design, use a print for Fabric C that blends well with itself.*

Echo Variation 5

Echo Variation 6

Mic's Musings: *Too many times, orange is only used once. Try using it twice—just make sure to use different shades.*

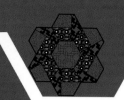

Rototiller

Be sure to read *General Supplies, English Paper Piecing Instructions*, and *Pieced Hexie Basting Instructions* before you start.

These instructions are for piecing 6 – 3 ½" squares for each rosette. The center hexagon is a solid fabric. No piecing instructions are needed: just use a 3 ½" square.

Fabric Orientation Guide

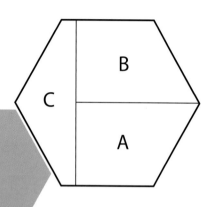
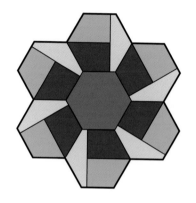
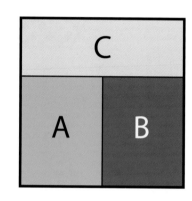

Material Needed for 1 Square

- Fabric A: 2" x 2 ½"
- Fabric B: 2" x 2 ½"
- Fabric C: 1 ½" x 3 ½"

Fabric Preparation

- Sew A to B.
- Sew that unit to a C.

OR

Material Needed for 6 Squares

- Fabric A: 2" x 16"
- Fabric B: 2" x 16"
- Fabric C: (6) 1 ½" x 3 ½"

Fabric Preparation

Important: Trim pieced seams to ⅛" after each one is sewn. This will reduce bulk for basting.

- Sew the strips together lengthwise in an A-B pattern.

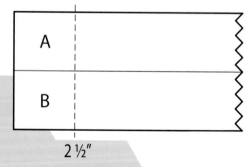

- Cut the A-B strip into 2 ½" segments.
- Sew the C strips onto the A-B unit. Be sure to orient the A-B unit the same way for all squares.

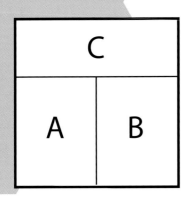

3 ½" Rototiller sewn square

Paper Preparation

Baste the sewn square to the paper pattern. Perfect alignment is important; mark your paper hexagon with the alignment guides shown. Use a sharp pointed pencil or fine tip pen to mark lines. To mark accurately, angle your marking instrument tip into the groove of the ruler and paper.

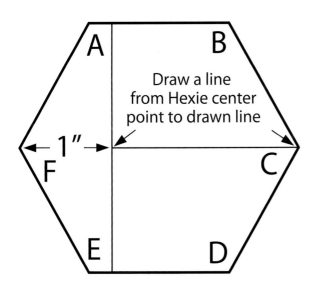

Rototiller Alignment Guides

Note: For this symmetrical block, place a paper Hexie in front of you and label the corners (A through F) as shown on the guide.

- Measure 1" to the right of corner F and draw a line vertically.
- Draw a line horizontally from corner C to the previously drawn line.

Assembly

- Place the sewn square with the seam side facing up.
- Place the marked paper pattern on top of the sewn square with markings facing up.
- Line up the sewn seams and paper marks. *Note: Push a pin through one or 2 of the corners of the center square to line up with drawn guideline square. Carefully pin once in the center, securing the sewn square to the paper.*
- Trim away excess fabric, leaving a generous ¼" on each side for basting.
- Baste the sewn square to the paper hexagon, using a running stitch. *Start your basting on an edge with a seam to secure.*
- **Do not** remove the pin until at least 3 sides are basted.

Rototiller Original

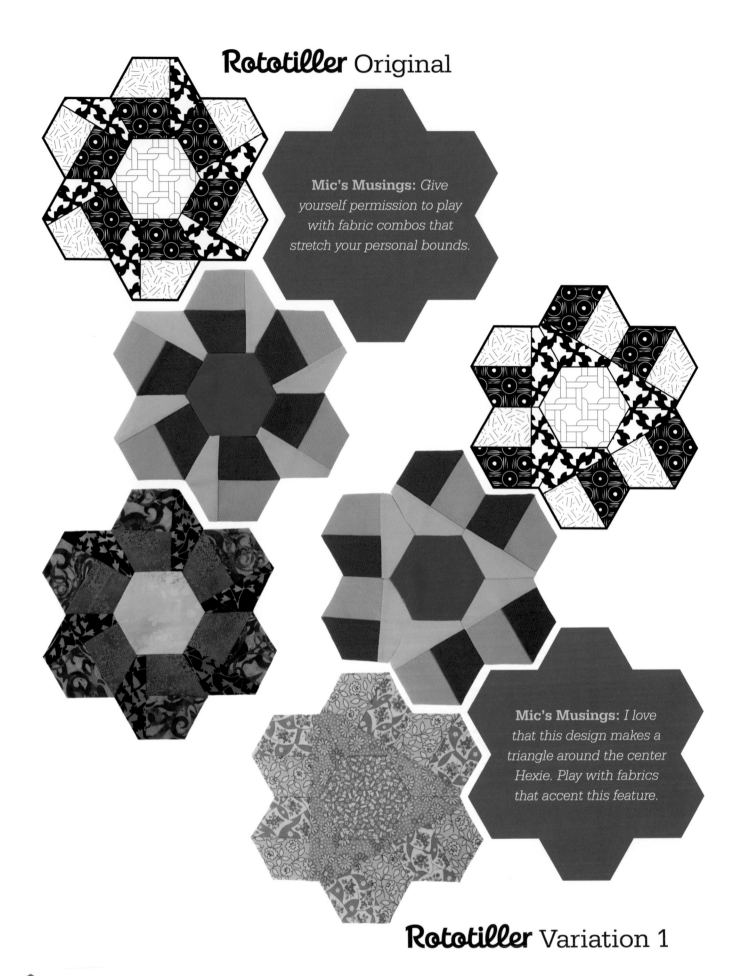

Mic's Musings: *Give yourself permission to play with fabric combos that stretch your personal bounds.*

Mic's Musings: *I love that this design makes a triangle around the center Hexie. Play with fabrics that accent this feature.*

Rototiller Variation 1

Rototiller Variation 2

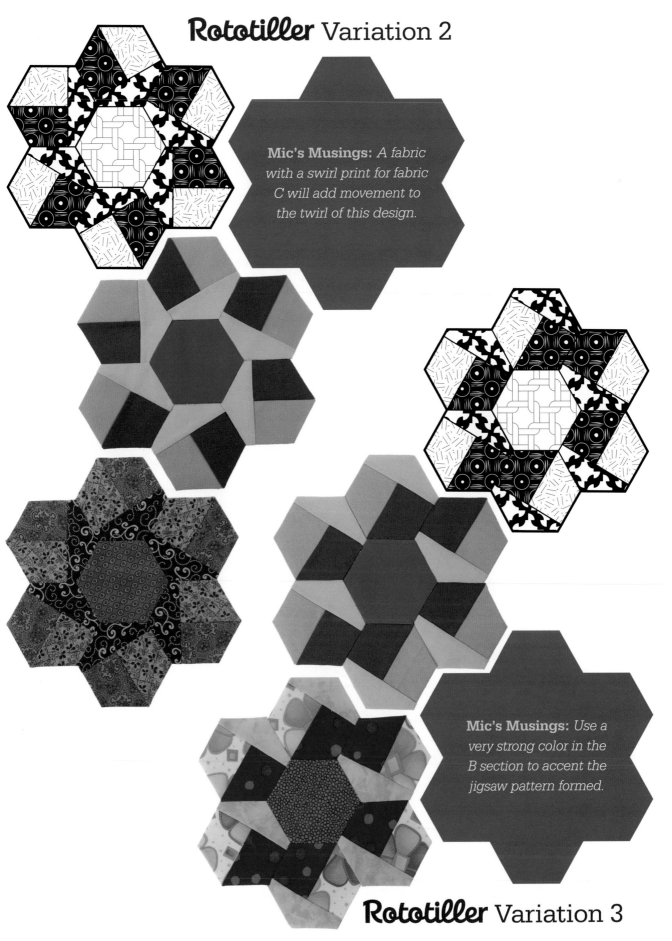

Mic's Musings: *A fabric with a swirl print for fabric C will add movement to the twirl of this design.*

Mic's Musings: *Use a very strong color in the B section to accent the jigsaw pattern formed.*

Rototiller Variation 3

Rototiller Variation 4

Mic's Musing: *When using two different reds in a design, make sure they are of different hues so they stand apart and don't blend.*

Mic's Musings: *Small scale stripes with a bit of wave in their design really make these V designs sing.*

Rototiller Variation 5

Rototiller Variation 6

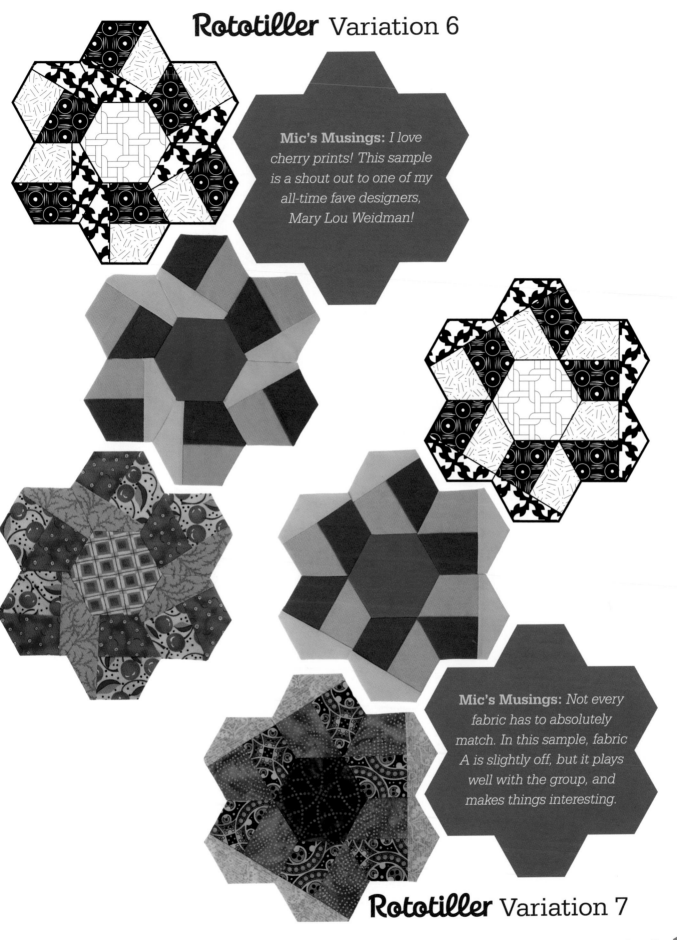

Mic's Musings: *I love cherry prints! This sample is a shout out to one of my all-time fave designers, Mary Lou Weidman!*

Mic's Musings: *Not every fabric has to absolutely match. In this sample, fabric A is slightly off, but it plays well with the group, and makes things interesting.*

Rototiller Variation 7

Rototiller Variation 8

Mic's Musings: *I purposely did not center the daisy print. I wanted the viewer to know it's daisies but didn't want it to be polarizing.*

Beaker

Be sure to read General Supplies, English Paper Piecing Instructions, and Pieced Hexie Basting Instructions before you start.

These instructions are for piecing 6 – 3 ½" squares for each rosette. The center hexagon is a solid fabric. No piecing instructions are needed: just use a 3 ½" square.

Fabric Orientation Guide

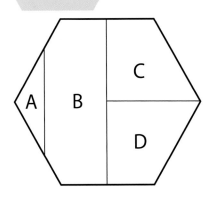
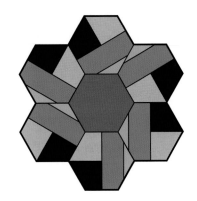
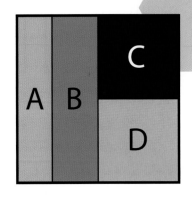

Material Needed for 1 Square

- Fabric A: 1" x 3 ½"
- Fabric B: 1 ½" x 3 ½"
- Fabric C: 2" x 2"
- Fabric D: 2" x 2"

Fabric Preparation

- Sew A lengthwise to B.
- Sew C to D.
- Sew A-B across the lengthwise edge of the C-D unit.
- Make sure the orientation is correct before sewing.

OR

Material Needed for 6 Squares

- Fabric A: 1" x 22"
- Fabric B: 1 ½" x 22"
- Fabric C: 2" x 13"
- Fabric D: 2" x 13"

Fabric Preparation

Important: Trim pieced seams to ⅛" after each one is sewn. This will reduce bulk for basting.

- Sew the A and B strips together lengthwise in an A-B pattern.

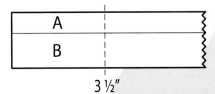

3 ½"

- Cut the A-B strip into 3 ½" segments.
- Sew C and D together lengthwise in a C-D pattern.

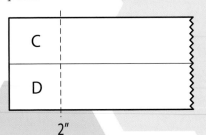

2"

- Cut the C-D strip into 2" segments.
- Sew A-B onto the lengthwise edge of the C-D unit.

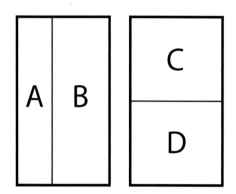

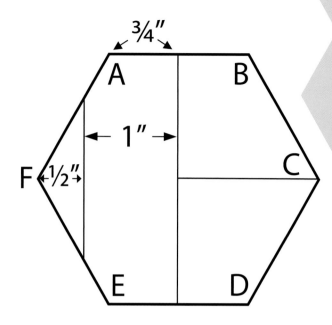

- Make sure the orientation is correct before you stitch.

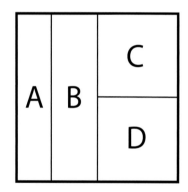

3 ½" Beaker sewn square

Paper Preparation

Baste the sewn square to the paper pattern. Perfect alignment is important; mark your paper hexagon with the alignment guides shown. Use a sharp pointed pencil or fine tip pen to mark lines. To mark accurately, angle your marking instrument tip into the groove of the ruler and paper.

Beaker Alignment Guides

Note: For this symmetrical block, place a paper Hexie in front of you and label the corners (A through F) as shown on the guide.

- Measure ½" to the right of corner F and draw a line vertically.
- Measure 1" from the drawn line and draw a second line vertically. This line will be ¾" to the right of corners A and E.
- Draw a horizontal line from corner C to the second drawn line.

Assembly

- Place the sewn square with the seam side facing up.
- Place the marked paper pattern on top of the sewn square with markings facing up.
- Line up the sewn seams and paper marks. Carefully pin once in the center, securing the sewn square to the paper.
- Trim away excess fabric, leaving a generous ¼" on each side for basting.
- Baste the sewn square to the paper hexagon, using a running stitch. *Start your basting on an edge with a seam to secure.*
- **Do not** remove the pin until at least 3 sides are basted.

Beaker Original

Mic's Musings: *Plaid, polka dots and stripes can all play together!*

Mic's Musings: *The pinks and corals are just similar enough to hold hands in this rosette.*

Beaker Variation 1

Beaker Variation 2

Mic's Musings: *I like mixing old-fashioned florals with today's bold graphic prints.*

Mic's Musings: *Put your strongest fabric in section B for an eye-catching effect.*

Beaker Variation 3

Beaker Variation 4

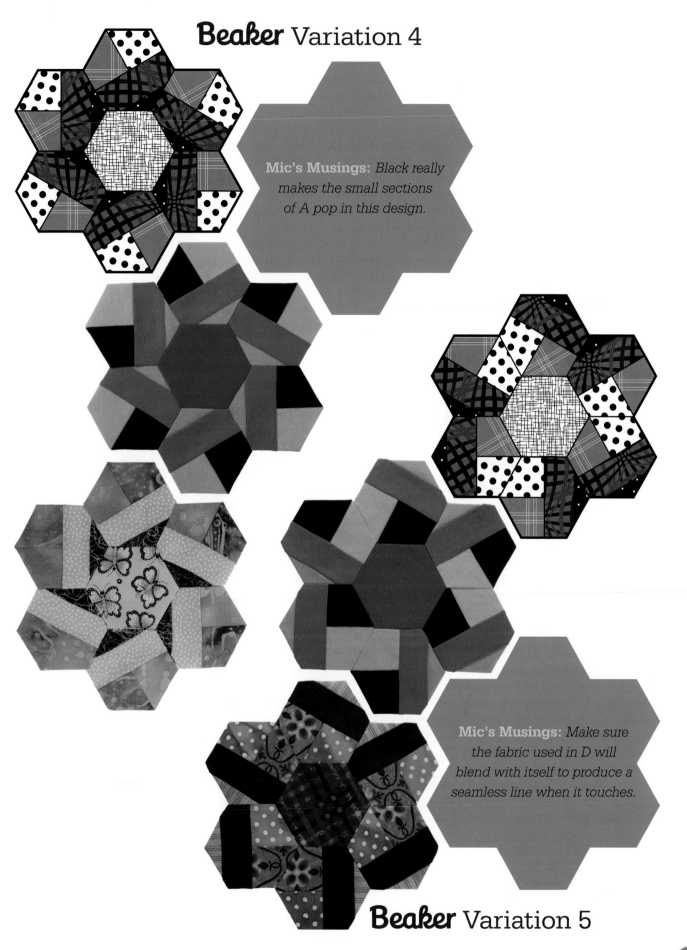

Mic's Musings: *Black really makes the small sections of A pop in this design.*

Mic's Musings: *Make sure the fabric used in D will blend with itself to produce a seamless line when it touches.*

Beaker Variation 5

Beaker Variation 6

Mic's Musings: *I can't help it—1930's prints make me smile. They are so light and fresh. And they give you the freedom to throw anything and everything into the mix.*

Mic's Musings: *I love the secondary pattern in the blue. Make sure to use a strong color in section C!*

Beaker Variation 7

50/50

Be sure to read General Supplies, English Paper Piecing Instructions, and Pieced Hexie Basting Instructions before you start.

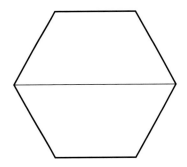

Material Needed for 1 Square

- ✪ Fabric A: 2" x 3 ½"
- ✪ Fabric B: 2" x 3 ½"

Fabric Preparation

- ✪ Sew A to lengthwise edge of B.

Material Needed for Multiple Squares

When a design needs more than one 50/50 and you wish to strip piece:

- ✪ Multiply the number of blocks needed by 3 ½" and add 1" to figure the length of 2" strip needed. (example: 8 blocks needed = 8 x 3 ½ =1 - 29" strip)
- ✪ Cut the same strip length for both A and B fabrics.
- ✪ Sew the strips together lengthwise in an A-B pattern.

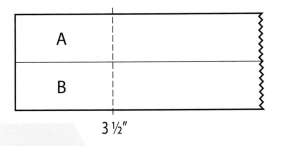

- ✪ Cut the A-B strip into 3 ½" segments.

50/50 Alignment Guides

- ✪ No need to mark your paper(s) for 50/50s. Just line up your seam, using any 2 opposing points on your Hexie. Trim. Baste.

Easy Peasey. You have made a 50/50 Pieced Hexie. Hex On!

Radicals

Take special note of the designs that follow: Boxed, Buzzsaw, Chop, Kilter, Layer and Scissors. I call these designs **Radicals**. These are **non-symmetrical quilt blocks**, so you mark your alignment guides in reverse. Remember: in all designs the paper lies on the back of the quilt block with the alignment guides facing you. Mark the paper in reverse so it all lines up correctly.

Asymmetrical
Designs

Take special note of the designs that follow: Boxed, Buzzsaw, Chop, Kilter, Layer and Scissors. These are non-symmetrical quilt blocks, so you mark your alignment guides in reverse. Remember: in all designs the paper lies on the back of the quilt block with the alignment guides facing you. Mark the paper in reverse so it all lines up correctly.

Boxed

Be sure to read General Supplies, English Paper Piecing Instructions, and Pieced Hexie Basting Instructions before you start.

These instructions are for piecing 6 – 3 ½" squares for each rosette. The center hexagon is a solid fabric. No piecing instructions are needed: just use a 3 ½" square.

Fabric Orientation Guide

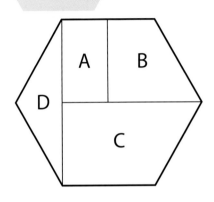
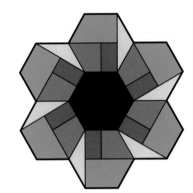
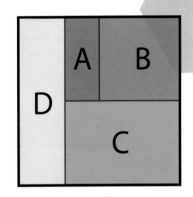

Material Needed for 1 Square

- Fabric A: 1 ¼" x 2"
- Fabric B: 2" x 2"
- Fabric C: (6) 2" x 2 ¾"
- Fabric D: 1 ¼" x 3 ½"

OR

Material Needed for 6 Squares

- Fabric A: 1 ¼" x 13"
- Fabric B: 2" x 13"
- Fabric C: 2" x 2 ¾"
- Fabric D: (6) 1 ¼" x 3 ½"

Fabric Preparation

Important: Trim pieced seams to ⅛" after each one is sewn. This will reduce bulk for basting.

- Sew the strips together lengthwise in an A-B pattern.
- Cut the A-B strip into 2" segments.

- Sew the C strips onto the A-B unit units. Be sure to orient the A-B unit the same for all the squares.
- Sew D across the unit on the C-A edge.

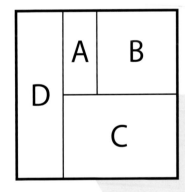

3 ½" Boxed sewn square

Paper Preparation

Baste the sewn square to the paper pattern. Perfect alignment is important; mark your paper hexagon with the alignment guides shown. Use a sharp pointed pencil or fine tip pen to mark lines.

To mark accurately, angle your marking instrument tip into the groove of the ruler and paper.

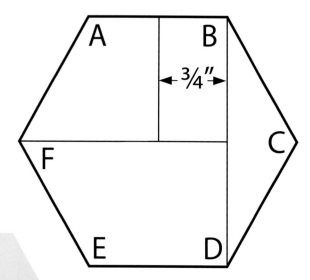

Boxed Alignment Guides

Note: For this asymmetrical block, draw the alignment guides in reverse of the finished block. Remember: you are working from the back. Label the corners (A through F) as shown on the guide.

- Draw a line vertically from corner B to corner D.

- Draw a line horizontally from corner F to the vertical line.

- Measure ¾" to the left of the vertical line in the upper half of the Hexie and draw a vertical line from the center to the top edge.

Assembly

- Place the sewn square with the seam side facing up.

- Place the marked paper pattern on top of the sewn square with markings facing up.

- Line up the sewn seams and paper marks. *Note: Push a pin through one or 2 of the corners of the center square to line up with drawn guideline square. Carefully pin once in the center, securing the sewn square to the paper.*

- Trim away excess fabric, leaving a generous ¼" on each side for basting.

- Baste the sewn square to the paper hexagon, using a running stitch. *Start your basting on an edge with a seam to secure.*

- **Do not** remove the pin until at least 3 sides are basted.

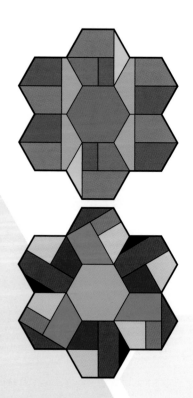

Boxed Original

Mic's Musings: This is a shout-out to my mini doxie Molly. All 9 pounds of her rules the roost! But note: I did make sure the dogs are all standing the same way.

Mic's Musings: Sure, you can mix polka dots and plaids! It's best if they are different colors.

Boxed Variation 1

Boxed Variation 2

Mic's Musings: Make sure the scale of print of your D fabric is small enough to be seen.

Mic's Musings: Purists will say the center color doesn't match ... but it works!

Boxed Variation 3

Boxed Variation 4

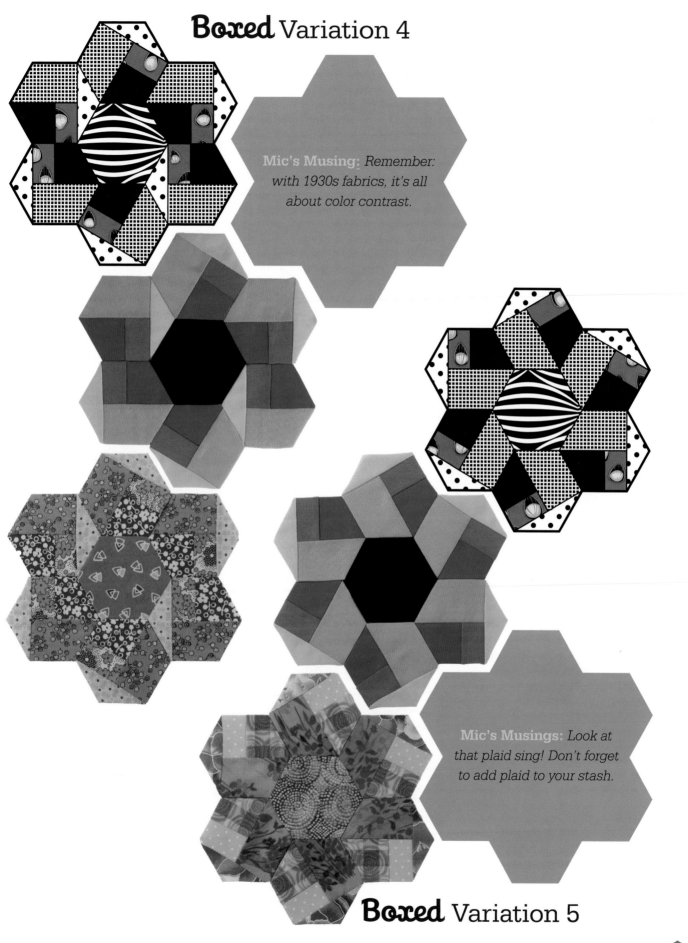

Mic's Musing: *Remember: with 1930s fabrics, it's all about color contrast.*

Mic's Musings: *Look at that plaid sing! Don't forget to add plaid to your stash.*

Boxed Variation 5

Boxed Variation 6

Mic's Musings: *When using two black fabrics, make sure the scale of prints is different so they don't blend.*

Mic's Musings: *Try using a stripe lengthwise in a triangular shape on the Hexie.*

Boxed Variation 7

Boxed Variation 8

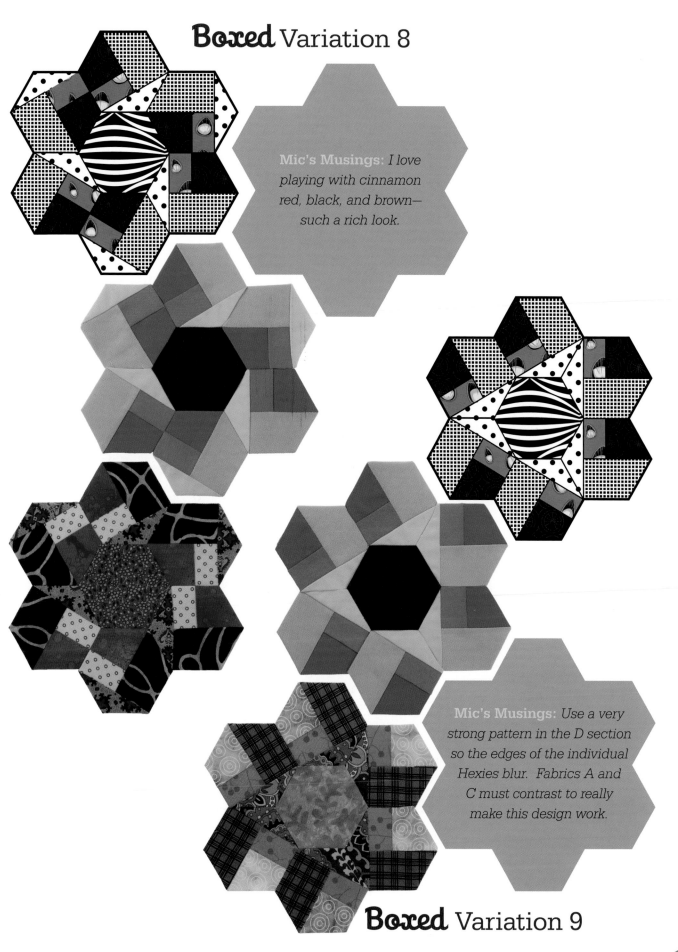

Mic's Musings: *I love playing with cinnamon red, black, and brown—such a rich look.*

Mic's Musings: *Use a very strong pattern in the D section so the edges of the individual Hexies blur. Fabrics A and C must contrast to really make this design work.*

Boxed Variation 9

Boxed Variation 10

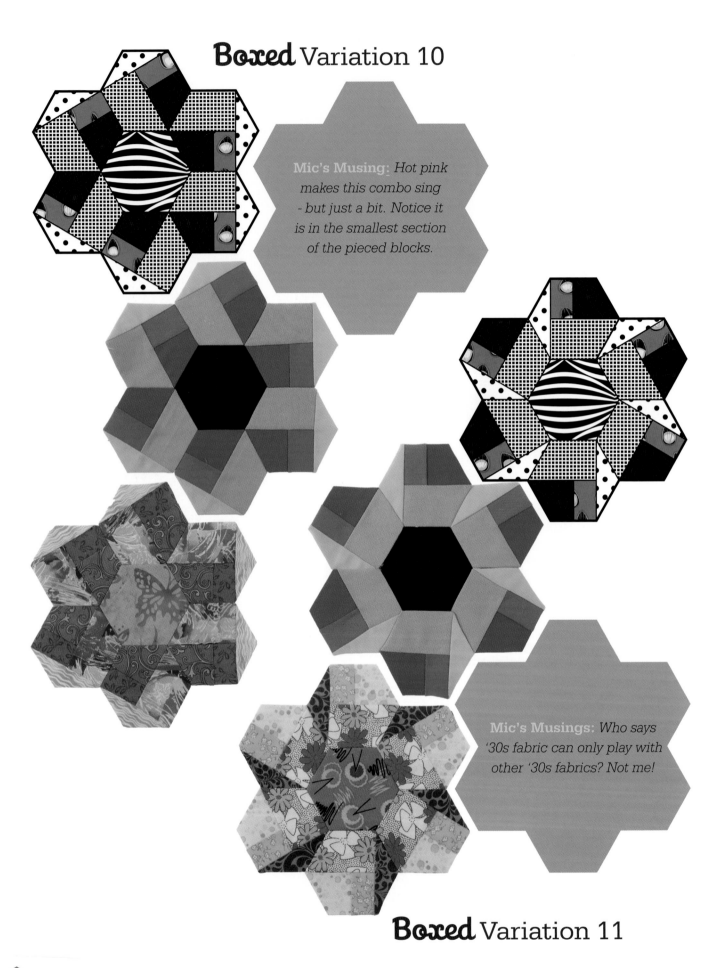

Mic's Musing: *Hot pink makes this combo sing - but just a bit. Notice it is in the smallest section of the pieced blocks.*

Mic's Musings: *Who says '30s fabric can only play with other '30s fabrics? Not me!*

Boxed Variation 11

Buzzsaw

Be sure to read General Supplies, English Paper Piecing Instructions, and Pieced Hexie Basting Instructions before you start.

These instructions are for piecing 6 – 3 ½" squares for each rosette. The center hexagon is a solid fabric. No piecing instructions are needed: just use a 3 ½" square.

Fabric Orientation Guide

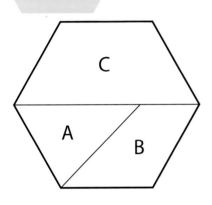

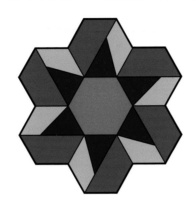

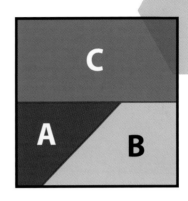

Material Needed for 1 Square

- ⊛ Fabric A: 2" x 2 1/2"
- ⊛ Fabric B: 2" x 3"
- ⊛ Fabric C: 2" x 3 1/2"
- ⬡

Fabric Preparation

Important: Trim pieced seams to ⅛" after each one is sewn. This will reduce bulk for basting.

- ⊛ Place B on top of A with right sides together. Sew together at a 45° angle.

- ⊛ Sew C onto the A/B unit.

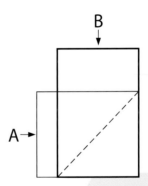

sew these lengths together make sure your AB rectangle is oriented correctly

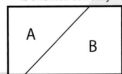

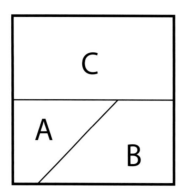

3 ½" Buzzsaw sewn square

Paper Preparation

Baste the sewn square to the paper pattern. Perfect alignment is important; mark your paper hexagon with the alignment guides shown. Use a sharp pointed pencil or fine tip pen to mark lines. To mark accurately, angle your marking instrument tip into the groove of the ruler and paper.

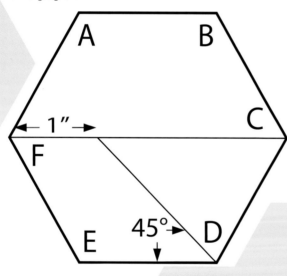

Buzzsaw Alignment Guides

Note: For this asymmetrical block, draw the alignment guides in reverse of the finished block. Remember: you are working from the back. Label the corners (A through F) as shown on the guide.

- ✸ Draw a line directly through the middle, using the center points as guides.

- ✸ Draw a line 45° from the lower right corner to the center line 1" from the left center corner.

Assembly

- ✸ Place the sewn square with the seam side facing up.

- ✸ Place the marked paper pattern on top of the sewn square with markings facing up.

- ✸ Line up the sewn seams and paper marks. *Note: Push a pin through one or 2 of the corners of the center square to line up with drawn guideline square. Carefully pin once in the center, securing the sewn square to the paper.*

- ✸ Trim away excess fabric, leaving a generous ¼" on each side for basting.

- ✸ Baste the sewn square to the paper hexagon, using a running stitch. *Start your basting on an edge with a seam to secure.*

- ✸ **Do not** remove the pin until at least 3 sides are basted.

Buzzsaw Original

Mic's Musings: *Don't be afraid to play with plaids. Just make sure to combine them with some solid-reading fabrics to give the eye somewhere to rest.*

Mic's Musings: *Fabrics can be in the same color family as long as there is a difference in print.*

Buzzsaw Variation 1

Buzzsaw Variation 2

Mic's Musings: *Make sure different scale prints are placed next to each other for contrast.*

Mic's Musings: *When like prints touch in a design, make sure the print blends into one large piece.*

Buzzsaw Variation 3

Buzzsaw Variation 4

Mic's Musings: *Sometimes a neutral is the pop you need to set strong fabrics apart.*

Mic's Musings: *Subtle can become dramatic when you add a black background fabric.*

Buzzsaw Variation 5

Buzzsaw Variation 6

Mic's Musings: *The scale of 1930s prints tends to be small, so make sure that your colors contrast to show the design.*

Mic's Musings: *Placing lights and darks next to each other can really add depth.*

Buzzsaw Variation 7

Chop

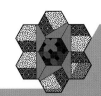

Be sure to read General Supplies, English Paper Piecing Instructions, and Pieced Hexie Basting Instructions before you start.

These instructions are for piecing 6 – 3 ½" squares for each rosette. The center hexagon is a solid fabric. No piecing instructions are needed: just use a 3 ½" square.

Fabric Orientation Guide

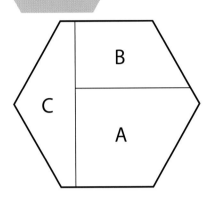

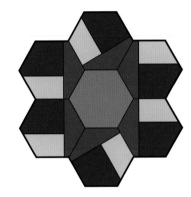

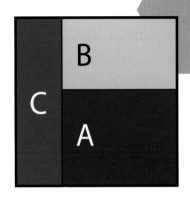

Material Needed for 1 Square

- Fabric A: 2 ¼" x 2 ½"
- Fabric B: 1 ¾" x 2 ½"
- Fabric C: 1 ½" x 3 ½"

Fabric Preparation

- Sew A lengthwise to B.
- Sew C across the lengthwise edge of the A-B unit.
- Make sure the orientation is correct before sewing.

OR

Material Needed for 6 Squares

- Fabric A: 2 ¼" x 16"
- Fabric B: 1 ¾" x 16"
- Fabric C: (6) 1 ½" x 3 ½"

Fabric Preparation

Important: Trim pieced seams to ⅛" after each one is sewn. This will reduce bulk for basting.

- Sew the A and B strips together lengthwise in an A-B pattern.

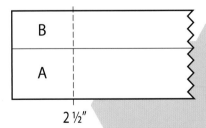

2 ½"

- Cut the A-B strip into 2 ½" segments.
- Sew C across the lengthwise edge of the A-B unit.
- Make sure the orientation is correct before sewing.

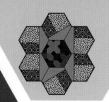

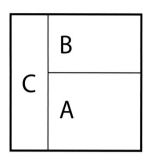

3 ½" Chop sewn square

Paper Preparation

Baste the sewn square to the paper pattern. Perfect alignment is important; mark your paper hexagon with the alignment guides shown. Use a sharp pointed pencil or fine tip pen to mark lines. To mark accurately, angle your marking instrument tip into the groove of the ruler and paper.

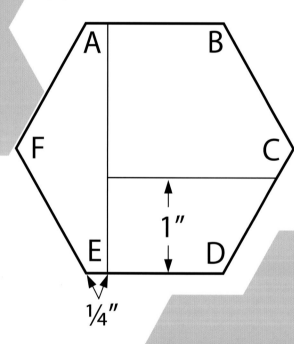

Layer Alignment Guides

Note: For this asymmetrical block, draw the alignment guides in reverse of the finished block. Remember: you are working from the back. Label the corners (A through F) as shown on the guide.

⊛ Measure ¼" to the right of corners A and E and draw a line vertically.

⊛ Measuring 1" from the bottom edge (between corners E and D), draw across from previous drawn line to the Hexie edge.

Assembly

⊛ Place the sewn square with the seam side facing up.

⊛ Place the marked paper pattern on top of the sewn square with markings facing up.

⊛ Line up the sewn seams and paper marks. Carefully pin once in the center, securing the sewn square to the paper.

⊛ Trim away excess fabric, leaving a generous ¼" on each side for basting.

⊛ Baste the sewn square to the paper hexagon, using a running stitch. *Start your basting on an edge with a seam to secure.*

⊛ **Do not** remove the pin until at least 3 sides are basted.

Chop Original

Mic's Musings: *Definitely choose a strong fabric for the C section to show off the center zigzag pattern.*

Mic's Musings: *Using a white or neutral fabric (usually regarded as a background fabric) gives the other fabrics an illusion of floating.*

Chop Variation 1

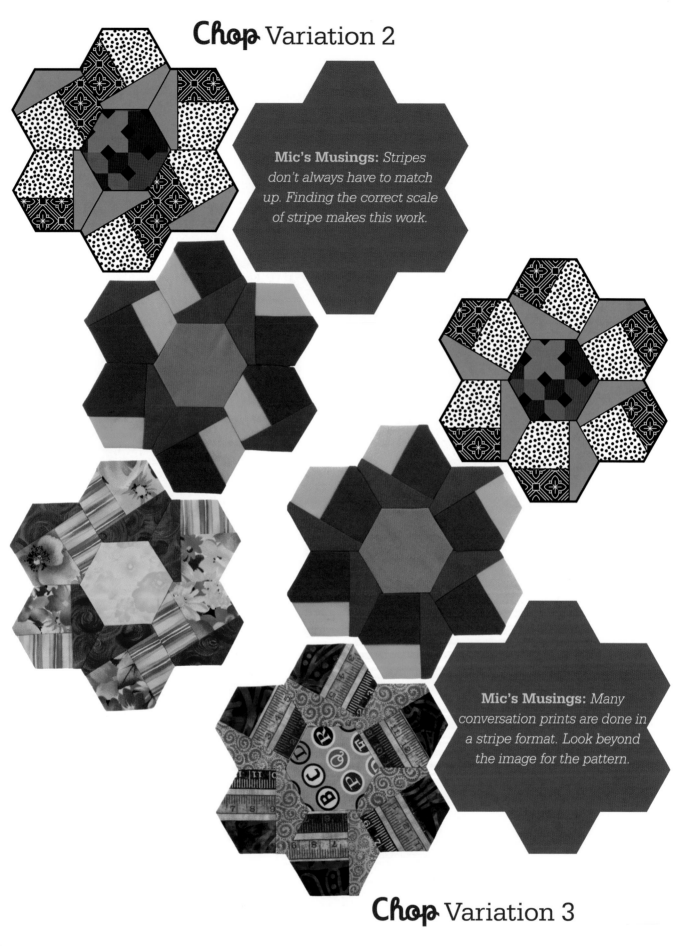

Chop Variation 2

Mic's Musings: *Stripes don't always have to match up. Finding the correct scale of stripe makes this work.*

Mic's Musings: *Many conversation prints are done in a stripe format. Look beyond the image for the pattern.*

Chop Variation 3

Chop Variation 4

Mic's Musings: *A Hexie print fabric in the center of a Hexie rosette makes me smile.*

Mic's Musings: *The center sunflower fabric is what I call a "packed floral" fabric. They usually show little or no background and bring a lot of movement to your project.*

Chop Variation 5

Chop Variation 6

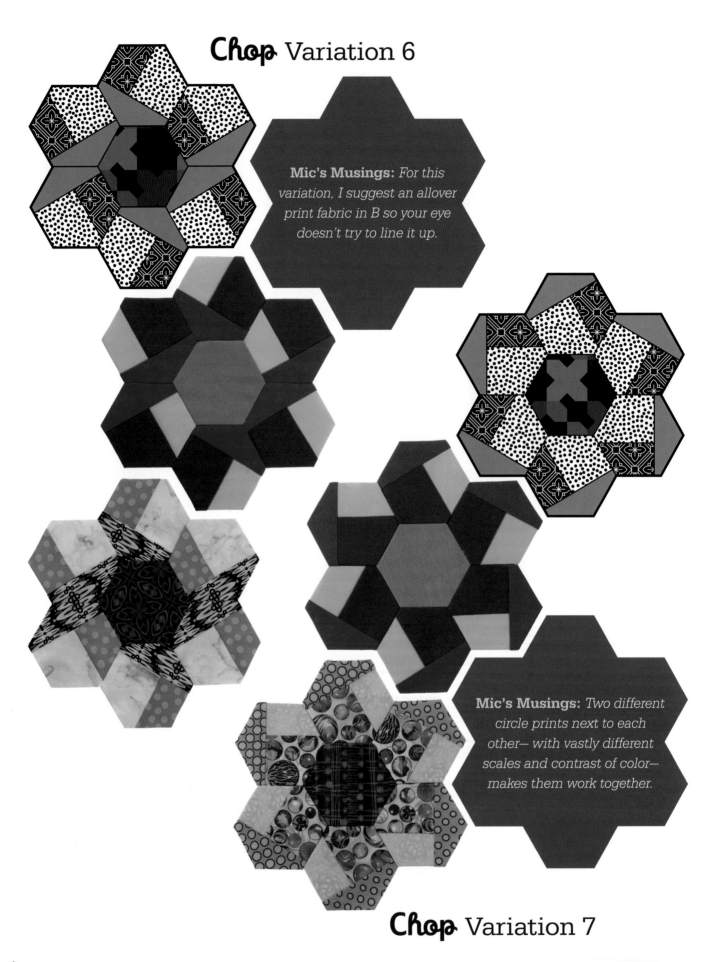

Mic's Musings: *For this variation, I suggest an allover print fabric in B so your eye doesn't try to line it up.*

Mic's Musings: *Two different circle prints next to each other— with vastly different scales and contrast of color— makes them work together.*

Chop Variation 7

Kilter

Be sure to read General Supplies, English Paper Piecing Instructions, and Pieced Hexie Basting Instructions before you start.

Note: *This design is a bit different.* These instructions are for piecing 6 – 3 1/2" x 3 3/4" rectangles for each rosette. The center hexagon is a solid fabric. No piecing instructions are needed: just use a 3 1/2" square.

Fabric Orientation Guide

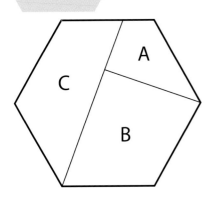

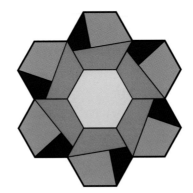

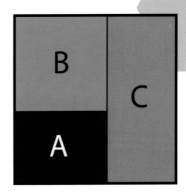

Material Needed for 1 Square

- ⬢ Fabric A: 1 ¾" x 2 ¼"
- ⬢ Fabric B: 2 ½" x 2 ¼"
- ⬢ Fabric C: 1 ¾" x 3 ¾"

Fabric Preparation

- ⬢ Sew A to the lengthwise edge of B.
- ⬢ Sew an A-B unit lengthwise to C.

OR

Material Needed for 6 Squares

- ⬢ Fabric A: 1 ¾" x 14 ½"
- ⬢ Fabric B: 2 ½" x 14 ½"
- ⬢ Fabric C: (6) 1 ¾" x 3 ¾"

Fabric Preparation

Important: Trim pieced seams to ⅛" after each one is sewn. This will reduce bulk for basting.

- ⬢ Sew the strips together lengthwise in an A-B pattern.

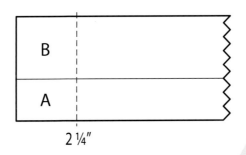

- ⬢ Cut A-B strip into 2 ¼" segments.
- ⬢ Sew C to the lengthwise edge of an A-B segment. Pay attention to the orientation of the A-B segment.

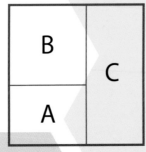

3 ½" x 3 ¾" Kilter sewn square

Paper Preparation

Baste the sewn square to the paper pattern. Perfect alignment is important; mark your paper hexagon with the alignment guides shown. Use a sharp pointed pencil or fine tip pen to mark lines. To mark accurately, angle your marking instrument tip into the groove of the ruler and paper.

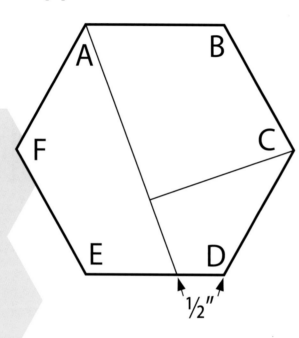

½"

Kilter Alignment Guides

Note: For this asymmetrical block, draw the alignment guides in reverse of the finished block. Remember: you are working from the back. Label the corners (A through F) as shown on the guide.

- ✹ Measure ½" to the right of corner D, draw a line from this point directly to corner A.

- ✹ Draw a line from C at a 90° angle to the previously drawn line.

Assembly

- ✹ Place the sewn square with the seam side facing up.

- ✹ Place the marked paper pattern on top of the sewn square with markings facing up.

- ✹ Line up the sewn seams and paper marks. Carefully pin once in the center, securing the sewn square to the paper.

- ✹ Trim away excess fabric, leaving a generous ¼" on each side for basting.

- ✹ Baste the sewn square to the paper hexagon, using a running stitch. *Start your basting on an edge with a seam to secure.*

- ✹ **Do not** remove the pin until at least 3 sides are basted.

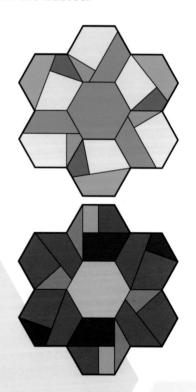

Kilter Original

Mic's Musings: *I for one am happy, happy, happy (nod to Phil) that grey taupes are in style right now. Fill your stash … they are wonderful with most everything.*

Mic's Musings: *If you haven't figured it out by now … I love my 1930s repros. It goes to show that you should never judge a quilter by their art quilts… deep inside, they may be a traditional chick too!*

Kilter Variation 1

Kilter Variation 2

Mic's Musings: *Sometimes, it's ok to have fabrics meld. Every quilt needs calm areas for the eye to rest.*

Mic's Musings: *A little dab of plaid!*

Kilter Variation 3

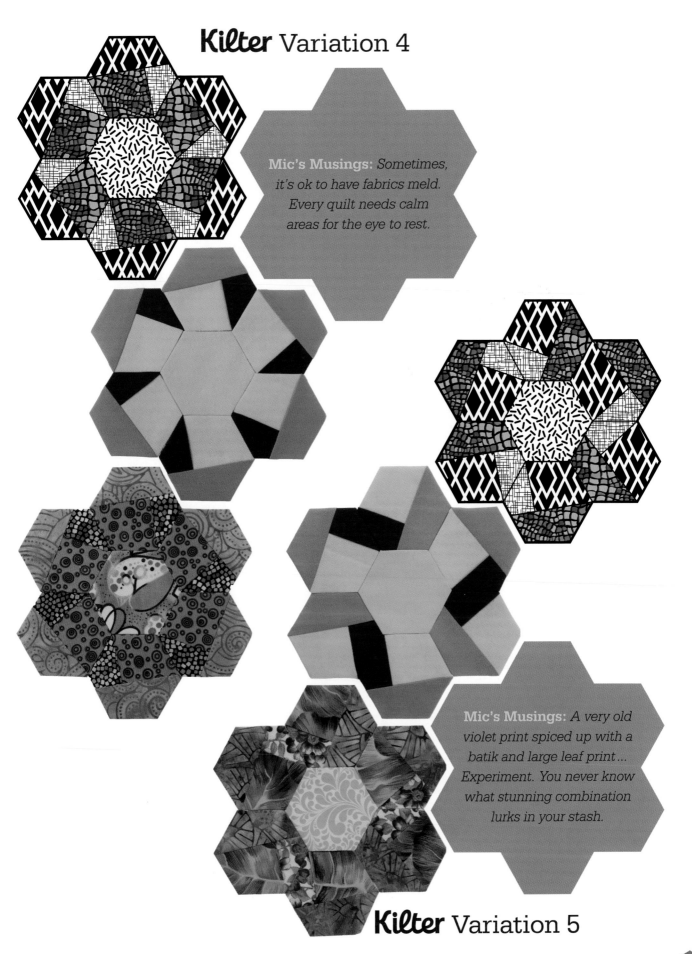

Kilter Variation 4

Mic's Musings: *Sometimes, it's ok to have fabrics meld. Every quilt needs calm areas for the eye to rest.*

Mic's Musings: *A very old violet print spiced up with a batik and large leaf print... Experiment. You never know what stunning combination lurks in your stash.*

Kilter Variation 5

Kilter Variation 6

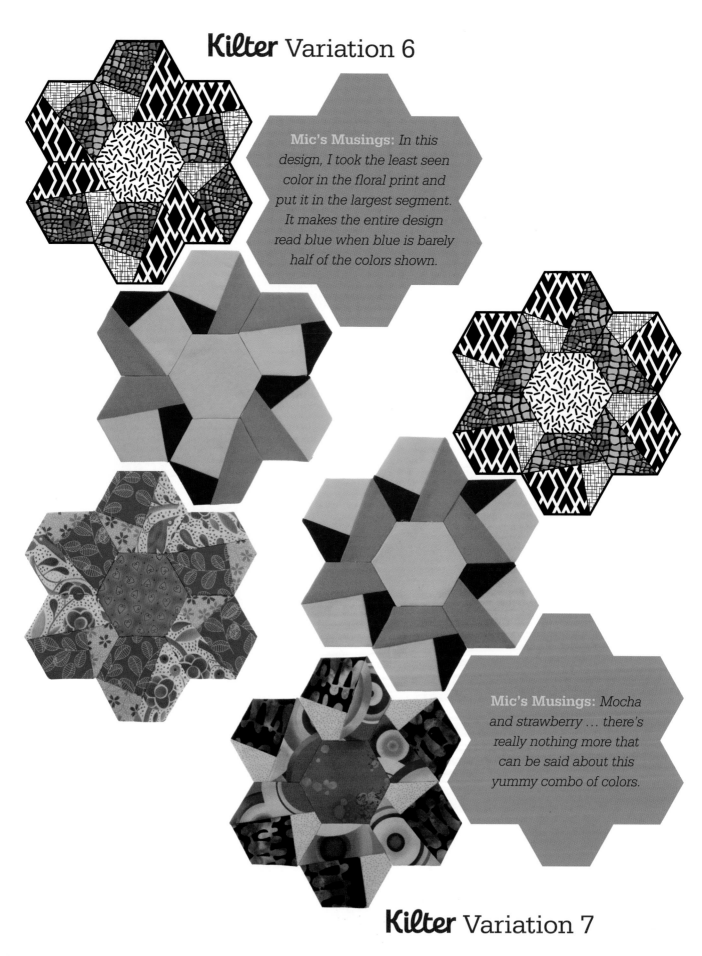

Mic's Musings: *In this design, I took the least seen color in the floral print and put it in the largest segment. It makes the entire design read blue when blue is barely half of the colors shown.*

Mic's Musings: *Mocha and strawberry ... there's really nothing more that can be said about this yummy combo of colors.*

Kilter Variation 7

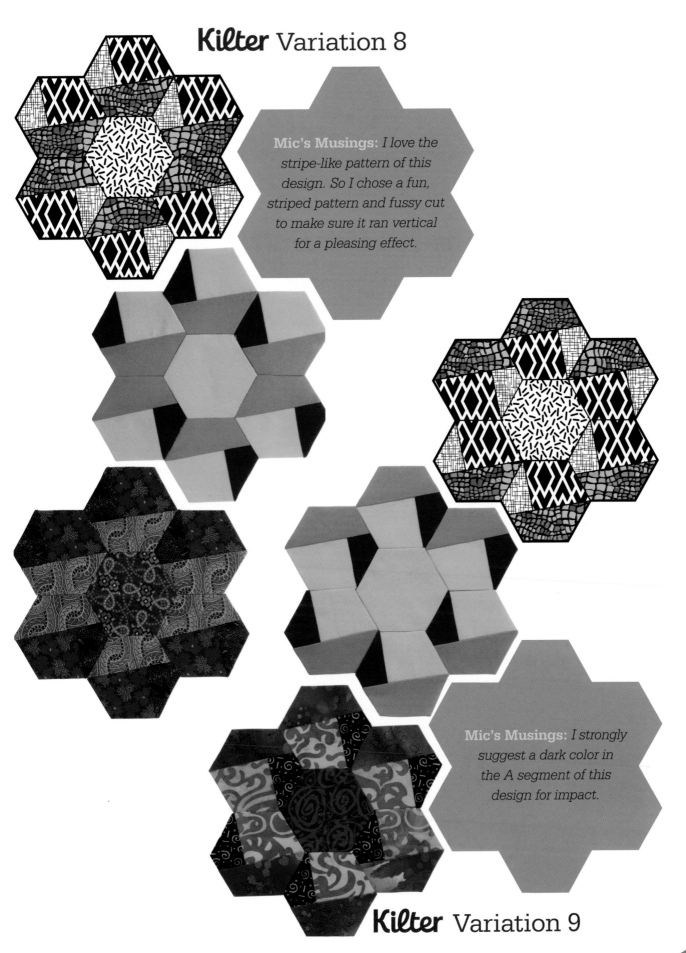

Kilter Variation 8

Mic's Musings: *I love the stripe-like pattern of this design. So I chose a fun, striped pattern and fussy cut to make sure it ran vertical for a pleasing effect.*

Mic's Musings: *I strongly suggest a dark color in the A segment of this design for impact.*

Kilter Variation 9

Layer

Be sure to read General Supplies, English Paper Piecing Instructions, and Pieced Hexie Basting Instructions before you start.

These instructions are for piecing 6 – 3 ½" squares for each rosette. The center hexagon is a solid fabric. No piecing instructions are needed: just use a 3 ½" square.

Fabric Orientation Guide

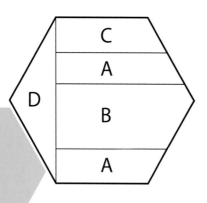 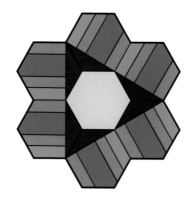 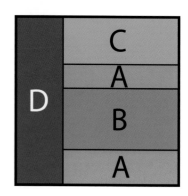

Material Needed for 1 Square

- Fabric A: 1 ¼" x 2 ¾" AND 1" x 2 ¾"
- Fabric B: 1 ½" x 2 ¾"
- Fabric C: 1 ¼" x 2 ¾"
- Fabric D: 1 ¼" x 3 ½"

Fabric Preparation

- Sew A (1 ¼" width piece of fabric) to the lengthwise edge of B.
- Sew an A-B unit lengthwise to A (1" width piece of fabric).
- Sew an A-B-A unit lengthwise to C along the 1" A side.
- Sew D across the top of the A-B-A-C unit. Make sure the orientation is correct before sewing.

OR

Material Needed for 6 Squares

- Fabric A: 1 ¼" x 17 ½" AND 1" x 17 ½"
- Fabric B: 1 ½" x 17 ½"
- Fabric C: 1 ¼" x 17 ½"
- Fabric D: (6) 1 ¼" x 3 ½"

Fabric Preparation

Important: Trim pieced seams to ⅛" after each one is sewn. This will reduce bulk for basting.

- Sew strips A (1 ¼" width piece) and B together lengthwise in an A-B pattern.
- Sew strip A (1" width piece) to the A/B unit along the lengthwise edge of B.
- Sew strip C to the A-B-A unit along the lengthwise edge of A (1" width).

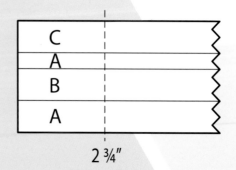

2 ¾"

- Cut the A-B-A-C strip into 2 ¾" segments.
- Sew D to the lengthwise edge of the A-B-A-C segment. Pay attention to orientation of the A-B-A-C segment.

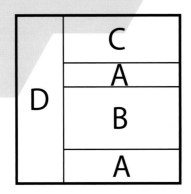

3 ½" Kilter sewn square

Paper Preparation

Baste the sewn square to the paper pattern. Perfect alignment is important; mark your paper hexagon with the alignment guides shown. Use a sharp pointed pencil or fine tip pen to mark lines. To mark accurately, angle your marking instrument tip into the groove of the ruler and paper.

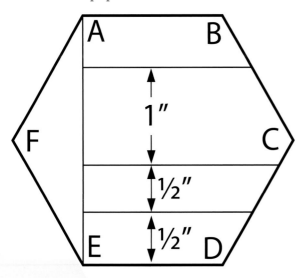

Layer Alignment Guides

Note: For this asymmetrical block, draw the alignment guides in reverse of the finished block. Remember: you are working from the back. Label the corners (A through F) as shown on the guide.

- Draw a line vertically from corner A to corner E.
- Measuring ½" from the bottom (edge between corners E and D) draw across from previous drawn line to the Hexie edge.
- Measure ½" from the previously drawn line and draw a line across.
- Measure 1" from the previously drawn line and draw a line across.

Assembly

- Place the sewn square with the seam side facing up.
- Place the marked paper pattern on top of the sewn square with markings facing up.
- Line up the sewn seams and paper marks. Carefully pin once in the center, securing the sewn square to the paper.
- Trim away excess fabric, leaving a generous ¼" on each side for basting.
- Baste the sewn square to the paper hexagon, using a running stitch. *Start your basting on an edge with a seam to secure.*
- **Do not** remove the pin until at least 3 sides are basted.

Layer Original

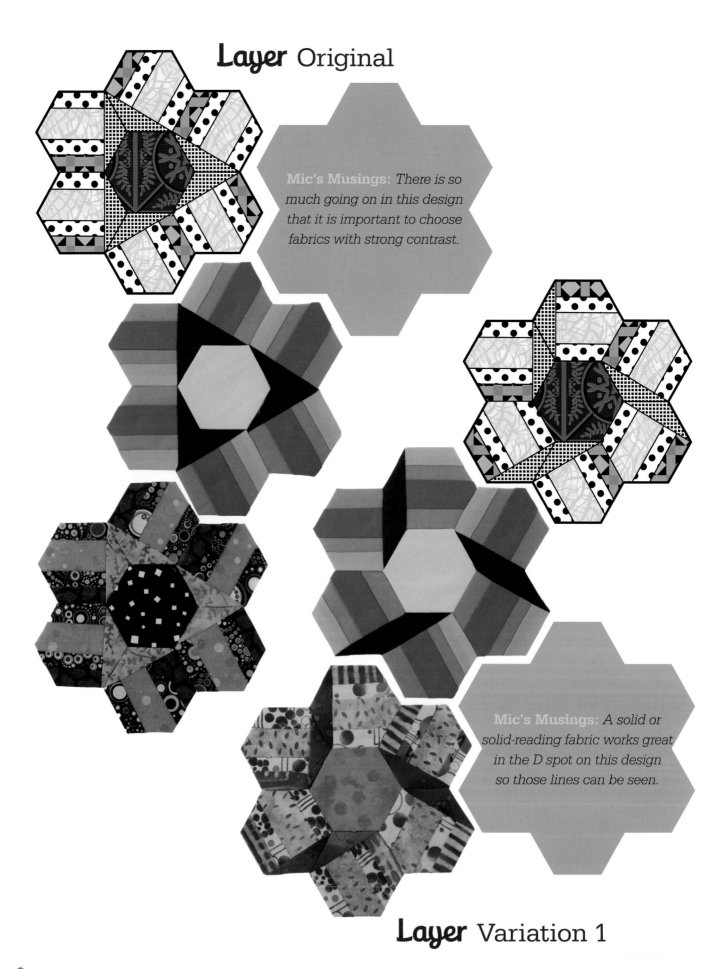

Mic's Musings: *There is so much going on in this design that it is important to choose fabrics with strong contrast.*

Mic's Musings: *A solid or solid-reading fabric works great in the D spot on this design so those lines can be seen.*

Layer Variation 1

Layer Variation 2

Mic's Musings: *The colors in this are very strong, yet with a soft sense too. This is because the fabrics blend (maybe a bit too much for my liking). Sometimes you need this here and there in a successful quilt.*

Mic's Musings: *Loving the chartreuse!*

Layer Variation 3

Layer Variation 4

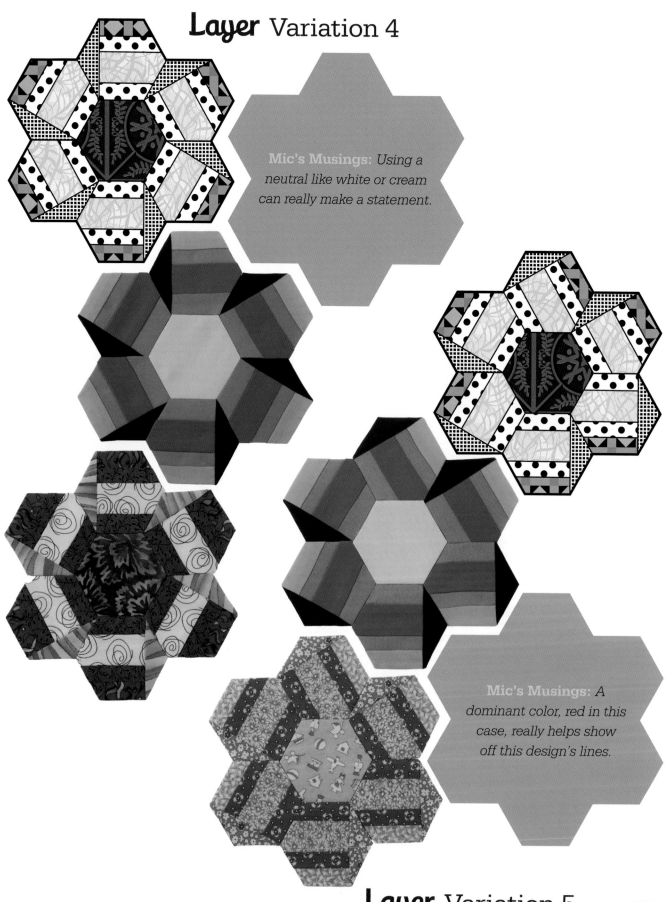

Mic's Musings: *Using a neutral like white or cream can really make a statement.*

Mic's Musings: *A dominant color, red in this case, really helps show off this design's lines.*

Layer Variation 5

Layer Variation 6

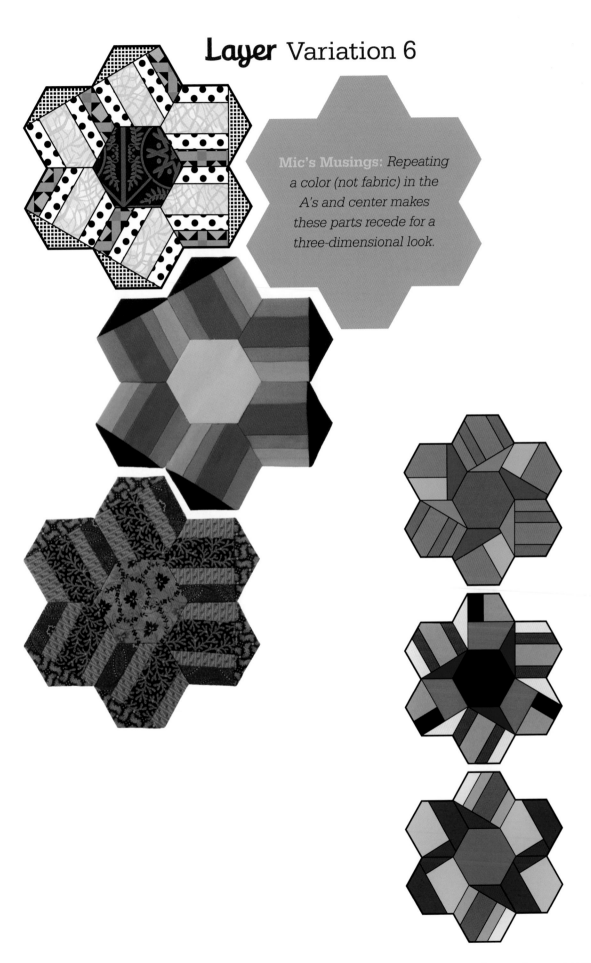

Mic's Musings: *Repeating a color (not fabric) in the A's and center makes these parts recede for a three-dimensional look.*

Scissors

Be sure to read General Supplies, English Paper Piecing Instructions, and Pieced Hexie Basting Instructions before you start.

These instructions are for piecing 6 – 3 ½" squares for each rosette. The center hexagon is a solid fabric. No piecing instructions are needed: just use a 3 ½" square.

Fabric Orientation Guide

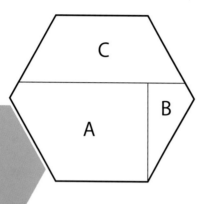 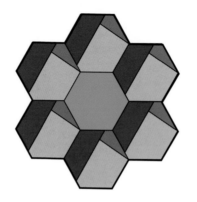 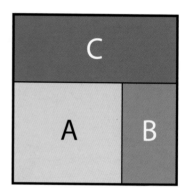

Material Needed for 1 Square

- ✪ Fabric A: 2 ¾" x 2 ¼"
- ✪ Fabric B: 1 ¼" x 2 ¼"
- ✪ Fabric C: 1 ¾" x 3 ½"

Fabric Preparation

- ✪ Sew A to the lengthwise edge of B.
- ✪ Sew an A/B unit lengthwise to C.

OR

Material Needed for 6 Squares

- ✪ Fabric A: 2 ¾" x 14 ½"
- ✪ Fabric B: 1 ¼" x 14 ½"
- ✪ Fabric C: (6) 1 ¾" x 3 ½"

Fabric Preparation

Important: Trim pieced seams to ⅛" after each one is sewn. This will reduce bulk for basting.

- ✪ Sew the strips together lengthwise in an A-B pattern.

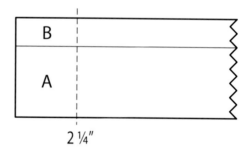

2 ¼"

- ✪ Cut A-B strip into 2 ¼" segments.
- ✪ Sew C to the lengthwise edge of the A-B segment. Pay attention to the orientation of the A-B segment.

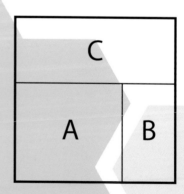

3 ½" Scissors sewn square

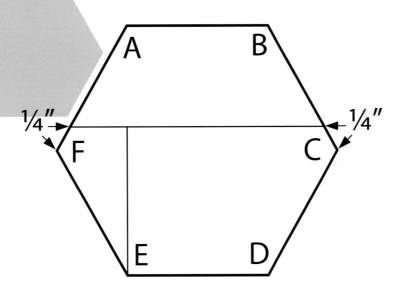

Paper Preparation

Baste the sewn square to the paper pattern. Perfect alignment is important; mark your paper hexagon with the alignment guides shown. Use a sharp pointed pencil or fine tip pen to mark lines. To mark accurately, angle your marking instrument tip into the groove of the ruler and paper.

Scissors Alignment Guides

Note: For this asymmetrical block, draw the alignment guides in reverse of the finished block. Remember: you are working from the back. Label the corners (A through F) as shown on the guide.

- ⊗ Measure ¼" upwards of corner F and C and mark, draw a line connecting these points.

Draw a line from E at 90° to the previously drawn line.

Assembly

- ⊗ Place the sewn square with the seam side facing up.

- ⊗ Place the marked paper pattern on top of the sewn square with markings facing up.

- ⊗ Line up the sewn seams and paper marks. Carefully pin once in the center, securing the sewn square to the paper.

- ⊗ Trim away excess fabric, leaving a generous ¼" on each side for basting.

- ⊗ Baste the sewn square to the paper hexagon, using a running stitch. *Start your basting on an edge with a seam to secure.*

- ⊗ **Do not** remove the pin until at least 3 sides are basted.

Scissors Original

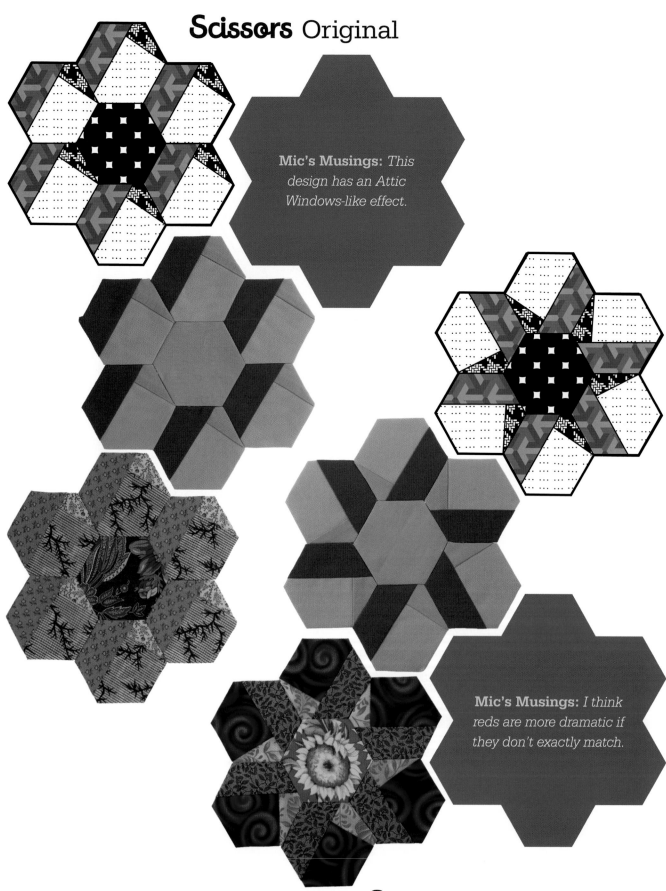

Mic's Musings: *This design has an Attic Windows-like effect.*

Mic's Musings: *I think reds are more dramatic if they don't exactly match.*

Scissors Variation 1

Scissors Variation 2

Mic's Musings: *A very abstract design, very modern. So, of course, I tried it out in 1930s reproduction fabrics.*

Mic's Musings: *I love the unique look of mixing reproduction fabrics (Civil War and '30s) with batiks and current prints.*

Scissors Variation 3

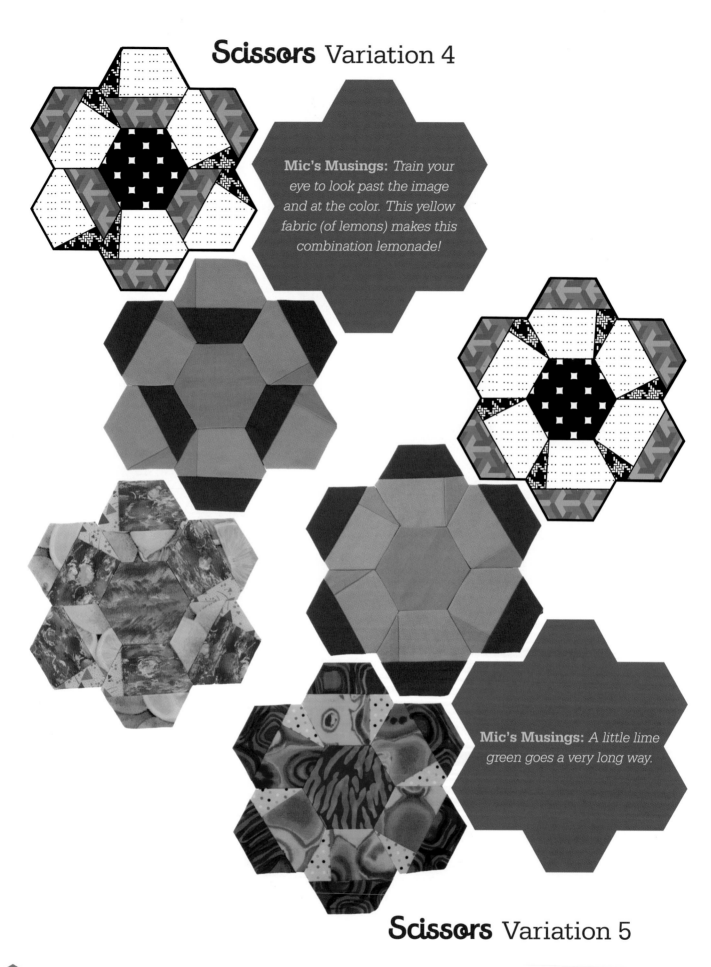

Scissors Variation 4

Mic's Musings: *Train your eye to look past the image and at the color. This yellow fabric (of lemons) makes this combination lemonade!*

Mic's Musings: *A little lime green goes a very long way.*

Scissors Variation 5

Scissors Variation 6

Mic's Musings: *Subtle and sophisticated is what I would call these color combinations.*

Mic's Musings: *Don't forget the babies in your life. They would love Pieced Hexie quilts too!*

Scissors Variation 7

Scissors Variation 8

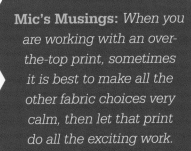

Mic's Musings: *When you are working with an over-the-top print, sometimes it is best to make all the other fabric choices very calm, then let that print do all the exciting work.*

Pieced Hexie
Stars

Bonnie

21" X 18 ½"

Bonnie is a Star design composed of these Pieced Hexies: Beaker, Lanes, 50/50, and Chop. Use a blank or traditional whole cloth Hexie for the center.

Hexie Guide

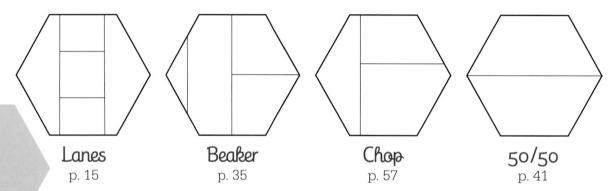

Lanes
p. 15

Beaker
p. 35

Chop
p. 57

50/50
p. 41

Materials Needed

- ✪ 37 – 1 ½" hexagon papers
- ✪ Various fabric scraps

Mark Alignment Guides

- ✪ 6 – Lanes
- ✪ 12 – Beaker
- ✪ 12 – Chop
- ✪ 6 – 50/50
- ✪ The center Hexie is blank/solid.

Design Recipe

This graphic shows the arrangement of the Hexie designs above.

- ✪ Red/center: Basic Hexie
- ✪ Green: 6 Beaker
- ✪ Blue: 6 Lanes – 6 - 50/50
- ✪ Orange: 12 Chop
- ✪ Black: 6 Beaker

Color your own star with this black and white graphic.

Cathy

21" X 18 ½"

Cathy is a Star design composed of these Pieced Hexies: Echo, Buzzsaw, Layer, and Rototiller. Use a blank or traditional whole cloth Hexie for the center.

Hexie Guide

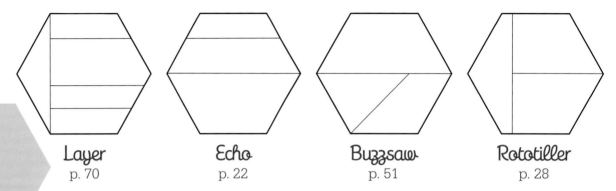

| Layer | Echo | Buzzsaw | Rototiller |
| p. 70 | p. 22 | p. 51 | p. 28 |

Materials Needed

- ✪ 37 – 1 ½" hexagon papers
- ✪ Various fabric scraps

Mark Alignment Guides

- ✪ 6 – Layer
- ✪ 12 – Echo
- ✪ 12 – Buzzsaw
- ✪ 6 – Rototiller

The center Hexie is blank/solid.

Design Recipe

This graphic shows the arrangement of the Hexie designs above.

- ✪ Red/center: Basic Hexie
- ✪ Green: 6 Echo
- ✪ Blue: 6 Echo – 6 Rototiller
- ✪ Orange: 12 Buzzsaw
- ✪ Black: 6 Layer

Color your own star with this black and white graphic.

Diane

21" X 18 ½"

Diane is a Star design composed of these Pieced Hexies: Beaker, Lanes, Buzzsaw, Boxed, and Chop. Use a blank or traditional whole cloth Hexie for the center.

Hexie Guide

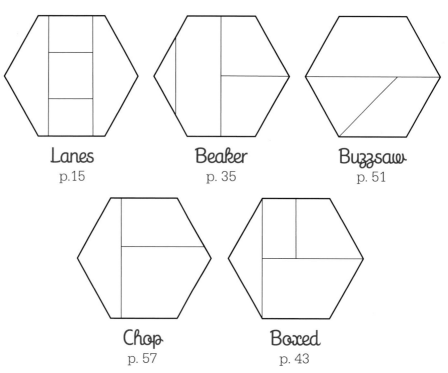

Lanes
p.15

Beaker
p. 35

Buzzsaw
p. 51

Chop
p. 57

Boxed
p. 43

Materials Needed

- ⊛ 37 – 1 ½" hexagon papers
- ⊛ Various fabric scraps

Mark Alignment Guides

- ⊛ 6 – Lanes
- ⊛ 12 – Beaker
- ⊛ 6 – Buzzsaw
- ⊛ 6 – Chop
- ⊛ 6 – Boxed

The center Hexie is blank/solid.

Design Recipe

This graphic shows the arrangement of the Hexie designs above.

- ⊛ Red: Basic Hexie
- ⊛ Green: 6 Lanes
- ⊛ Blue: 6 Boxed – 6 Buzzsaw
- ⊛ Orange: 12 Beaker
- ⊛ Black: 6 Chop

Color your own star with this black and white graphic.

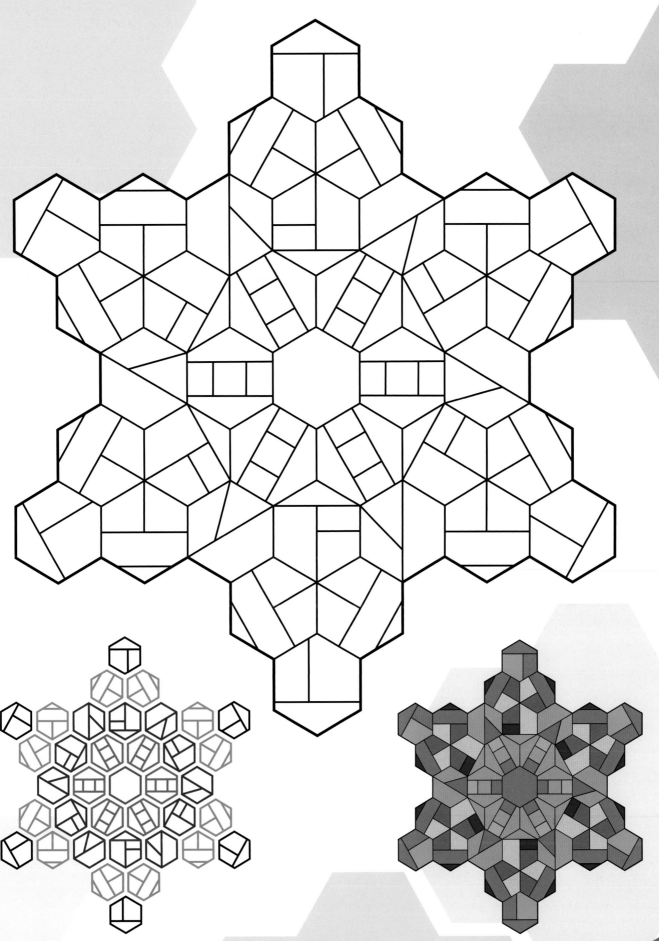

Elaine

21" X 18 ½"

Elaine is a Star design composed of these Pieced Hexies: Lanes, Echo, Buzzsaw, 50/50, and Rototiller. Use a blank or traditional whole cloth Hexie for the center.

Hexie Guide

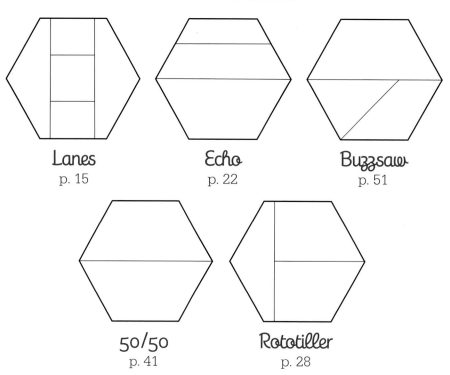

Lanes
p. 15

Echo
p. 22

Buzzsaw
p. 51

50/50
p. 41

Rototiller
p. 28

Materials Needed

- ✪ 37 – 1 ½" hexagon papers
- ✪ Various fabric scraps

Mark Alignment Guides

- ✪ 9 – Buzzsaw
- ✪ 3 – 50/50
- ✪ 6 – Lanes
- ✪ 6 – Echo
- ✪ 12 – Rototiller

The center Hexie is blank/solid.

Design Recipe

This graphic shows the arrangement of the Hexie designs above.

- ✪ Red: Basic Hexie
- ✪ Green: 3 Buzzsaw – 3 50/50
- ✪ Blue: 6 Lanes – 6 Echo
- ✪ Orange: 12 Rototiller
- ✪ Black: 6 Buzzsaw

Color your own star with this black and white graphic.

Linda

21" X 18 ½"

Linda is a Star design composed of these Pieced Hexies: Kilter, 50/50, Boxed, and Rototiller. Use a blank or traditional whole cloth Hexie for the center.

Hexie Guide

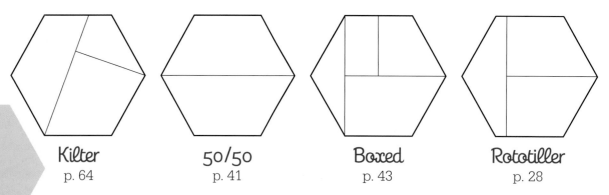

| Kilter | 50/50 | Boxed | Rototiller |
| p. 64 | p. 41 | p. 43 | p. 28 |

Materials Needed

- ✹ 37 – 1 ½" hexagon papers
- ✹ Various fabric scraps

Mark Alignment Guides

- ✹ 6 – Kilter
- ✹ 6 – 50/50
- ✹ 12 – Boxed
- ✹ 12 – Rototiller

The center Hexie is blank/solid.

Design Recipe

This graphic shows the arrangement of the Hexie designs above.

- ✹ Red/center: Basic Hexie
- ✹ Green: 6 Kilter
- ✹ Blue: 6 50/50 – 6 Boxed
- ✹ Orange: 12 Rototiller
- ✹ Black: 6 Boxed

Color your own star with this black and white graphic.

Maggie

21" X 18 ½"

Maggie is a Star design composed of these Pieced Hexies: Chop, Scissors, Echo and Layer. Use a blank or traditional whole cloth Hexie for the center.

Hexie Guide

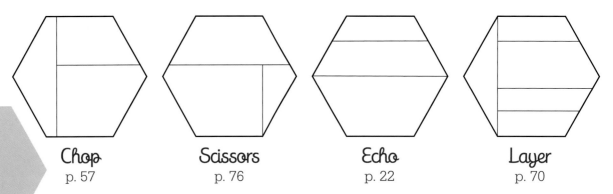

Chop
p. 57

Scissors
p. 76

Echo
p. 22

Layer
p. 70

Materials Needed

- ✪ 37 – 1 ½" hexagon papers
- ✪ Various fabric scraps

Mark Alignment Guides

- ✪ 10 – Chop
- ✪ 6 – Scissors
- ✪ 6 – Echo
- ✪ 14 – Layer

The center Hexie is blank/solid.

Design Recipe

This graphic shows the arrangement of the Hexie designs above.

- ✪ Red/center: Basic Hexie
- ✪ Green: 6 Scissors
- ✪ Blue: 6 Layer — 4 Chop — 2 Echo
- ✪ Orange: 8 Layer — 4 Echo
- ✪ Black: 6 Chop

Color your own star with this black and white graphic.

Resources

APQS – longarm machines and GEORGE! (my machine for quilting)
www.apqs.com

Bernina of America – sewing machine, of course
www.berninausa.com

Clover – needle threader
www.clover-usa.com

Colonial Need Company – needles and Prescenia Thread
www.colonialneedle.com

Electric Quilt – Boutique Collection of ALL designs in Pieced Hexies for easy designing
www.electricquilt.com

Paper Pieces – English paper piecing supplies
www.paperpieces.com

Stof Fabrics – background fabrics and staples
www.stof-dk.com

YLI Thread – silk thread
www.ylicorp.com